The Gifted Journey™

Five Transformative Steps
to Uncovering Your Unique Path

By Stephanie Moore

"Once the soul awakens, the search begins and you can never go back.

—John O'Donohue, Anam Cara, *A Book of Celtic Wisdom*

Inspired Forever Book Publishing

Dallas, Texas

The Gifted Journey:
Five Transformative Steps to Uncovering Your Unique Path

Inspired Forever Book Publishing™
"Bringing Inspiration to Life"
Dallas, Texas
(888) 403-2727

Printed in the United States of America

Library of Congress Control Number: 2018952396

ISBN-13: 978-0-9996258-8-0

Stephanie Moore
www.thegiftedjourney.com
stephanie@thegiftedjourney.com
(925) 980-7774

Praise for Stephanie Moore's
The Gifted Journey

The "wow" moment in this book is when you recognize that each day is a gift waiting to be opened and discovered. I strongly subscribe to Stephanie's thesis that our life journey should be used to uncover and emphasize our strengths—and to build upon these gifts for a more fulfilling and promising future. Executing this five-stage process will allow us to live the life that was always intended just for us.

I was a business leader for over thirty years, and as president and CEO of Eddie Bauer, I suffered a life-threatening stroke that changed my world and led me to embrace these stages. Using this process allowed me to discern how best to change my course, and how to apply my gifts to the faith world as executive director of stewardship and development at the Archdiocese of Seattle.

Through living my own life journey, I can readily embrace and endorse Stephanie's well laid out process. It is both refreshing and innovative—building on widely known and successful concepts for helping to find your true self. Her unique and easy-to-read format allows you to execute action points that help support your master life plan.

—Rick Fersch
Former president and CEO of Eddie Bauer and former executive director of stewardship and development at the Archdiocese of Seattle

Psychologist Carl Jung said, "The biggest challenge of mid-life is the question, 'What is my story?'" Imagine being able to control that story early in life, rather than just looking in the rearview mirror and trying to piece it together later. Stephanie Moore has given us the tools to do just that. Whether you are starting out life in high school or making major mid-life changes, this book is the tool belt that will help you construct your future. It is all here: self-assessment tools; exercises to understand your strengths and passions; and ways to evaluate where you fit into the world of work.

Stephanie's writing style is so accessible. She feels like an old friend who is being straight with you by letting you inside her own life-changing struggles. My favorite part was the doctor the young Stephanie consulted because of her stress and unhappiness. He told her, "Quit your job. It is killing you." Later in a different job, her new boss asked what turned her on. Her response: "I like to teach and lead groups." Her boss said, "Well, then, guess we need to get you in front of groups." Her future opened up in that moment.

If you are struggling to understand how your past can chart your future happiness, read this book. Do the exercises. Put it into action. Then write a thank you note to Stephanie. Sigmund Freud once said, "The boy is father to the man." With *The Gifted Journey*, you can own that process.

Strap on this tool belt.

—Fredrick Gilbert, Ph.D.
Let'er Rip Productions
Author, *Speaking UP: Surviving Executive Presentations*

The Gifted Journey is an amazing contribution! As Stephanie shares from her own Gifted Journey, she will lead you to discover your own conscious competence at whatever time in your life you meet her invitation. When individuals truly work in their strengths zone, it feels just right to them and others like it too. One can feel Stephanie's joy and pleasure—not only in her own life's multifaceted talent discoveries, but also in her day-to-day experience of living them out. Walk with Stephanie through her 5-D strategy for life's journey. Find a **gift** on every page as you learn, love, and live your Gifted Journey.

—Jo Ann Miller, OSF
Strengths Development Center, Milwaukee, WI
Former 40-year Gallup employee
Co-author, *Teach with Your Strengths*

Stephanie Moore's *The Gifted Journey* serves as your personal archaeologist. As you proactively become a searcher of clues, a seeker of patterns, and a creator for your own fulfilled future, you find the path to your own career satisfaction. With assessments, tools, and exercises, your story unfolds in a magical way.

—Mary McGlynn
President and vice president of learning, development, and research at PowerSpeaking, Inc.

In loving memory of our grandmother, Dorothy "Dot" Spoerl, who recognized the unique beauty in each person she met.

"Love is like a butterfly: it goes wherever it pleases and pleases wherever it goes."

—Author Unknown

ACKNOWLEDGEMENTS

This book has been a five-year labor of love and is based on a thirty-year journey. As with any great journey, it is made up of the wonderful people I have met on my path who have impacted me in marvelous and significant ways. My personal transformation lies in these amazing individuals who over the years have enlightened, taught, mentored, and encouraged me. My gratitude goes beyond simple words of thank you. You have forever enhanced my journey.

First I'd like to acknowledge the two instrumental "Lindas" in my life. The first is Linda Jackson, my high school counselor who one day pulled me into her office and declared that I was going to college—a path that I had yet to consider. Her persuasive nature made me realize that this was a path worth taking. The second is Linda Doll, my first true "developmental" manager (you will read more about her in the book). Linda helped me realize that doing what I loved was key to having a meaningful career and life.

Next, words cannot express adequately the two women who took this five-year dream and made it a reality: Michelle Morse and her company at Inspire On Purpose Publishing, along with Wendy Cornett, editor extraordinaire. Thank you both for your love, care, and the magical editing of this book, all of which went beyond my wildest hopes and dreams. And to graphic artist Rick Rodriquez, thank you for this stunning cover and somehow intuitively knowing that butterflies play a significant role in our family.

To all those pioneers who have chartered the strengths path and led this movement in self-development. I specifically would like to thank Dr. Donald Clifton, Jim Clifton, Al Winseman, Jo Ann Miller, Rick and Patti Fersch, Rev. Bill Hanson, Rev. Ron Schmit, Dr. Rick Gilbert, Mary McGlynn, Dr. W. Craig Gilliam, Leisa Anslinger, Tara Bergen, Donna Stone, and Andrea McCann. You have each played a unique and significant role in my journey.

To all my friends and colleagues (you know who you are), thank you to each and every one of you for being such a special part of my journey. Please know that I love you and will be forever grateful for what you have meant in my life.

To my family, especially my mother Mary Ann, who taught her children the gift of perseverance in the toughest of times and through it all to always find humor in the smallest of things. To my grandparents Dorothy and Bud, who loved us, raised us, and gave us a strong foundation on which to stand. To my dear siblings and their families—my sister Chris Harrington, my brother Keith Bloss—whose love and support has been one of the biggest constants and gifts on my journey. A special shout out to all my amazing nieces and nephews—you give me great hope for the future.

To my spiritual director Frances Hodge, you've been with me every step of this Gifted Journey process. You have been my rock and spiritual leader, and I can't thank you enough for your ongoing love and encouragement (even during those times when the path was not clear). Thank you for never giving up.

Last, to my family. To my husband Tom, who has journeyed alongside me every step of the way. I could not have picked a better travel partner, and I will forever thank you for your constant love, wisdom, and encouragement. To my amazing son Brian and his wife Amanda, your love and dedication to each other, to our family, and to making the world a better place is a testament to this Gifted Journey process. To my youngest son Andrew, who, in his amazing and intuitive way, encouraged me early on to write this book, saying, "Do it because you can, and if you don't, no one else will." You have all been my inspiration. Thank you. I love you all.

TABLE OF CONTENTS

FOREWORD

There is a scene from *Joe vs. the Volcano*—a 1990 film by John Patrick Shanley that stars Tom Hanks and Meg Ryan—that provides insight into the human condition. It's a beautiful star-lit night on a yacht in the middle of the Pacific Ocean, and Joe (Tom Hanks) and Patricia (Meg Ryan) are having a philosophical after-dinner discussion. At one point, Patricia says to Joe, "My father says that almost the whole world is asleep. Everybody you know, everybody you see, everybody you talk to. He says that only a few people are awake and they live in a state of constant, total amazement." There is a simple yet profound truth to those words, and the remedy lies in discovering who you are and then living an authentic life—a life of "constant, total amazement."

Most people do not live their lives with intentionality; they float through life, drifting aimlessly—or as is often the case, buffeted by the storms of life and tossed about on the restless and unrelenting sea. Life doesn't have to be that way, and Stephanie Moore uses her life experiences to provide readers with a practical alternative, a way to live life on purpose. In the following chapters, Stephanie outlines a practical blueprint to fully live your one and only life: *Discover* who you are, *Discern* your best path forward, *Dream* of what you might become, *Design* your best life, and then . . . *Do* it!

In my eighteen years as a leadership consultant with Gallup, I have had the privilege of coaching executives, managers, and individual contributors in a wide range of organizations—healthcare, financial services, higher education, and governmental agencies to name but a few. I am philosophically attuned to coaching, which begins with the premise that you are not broken, and I am not here to fix you. You have everything you need inside of you to achieve your outcomes and meet your challenges. My role as a coach is to draw out and help you apply what you already have. *The Gifted Journey* provides practical actions to discover and apply what is already inside of you. Quite simply:

> Don't try to put in what God left out.
> Instead, try to draw out what God put in.
> That is a lifetime's worth of work.

As you read this book and apply its principles, you will be relying on and developing your God-given talents—what "God put in"— and living the life you were meant to live. I wish you well as you begin your Gifted Journey!

Albert L. Winseman, D.Min.
Co-author, *Living Your Strengths*
September 2018

INTRODUCTION

What is a Gifted Journey?

The Gifted Journey is different. This is not a one-size-fits-all, "here's what's wrong with you" approach to self-improvement. *The Gifted Journey* is designed to help you uncover and emphasize your strengths—your gifts—and build upon those gifts for a more fulfilling and promising future. *The Gifted Journey* requires your participation—your involvement—along the way. Your engagement is what makes the journey yours and yours alone.

The Gifted Journey is about realizing your gifts, understanding who you are, and taking stock of what has gotten you where you are today using the appreciative inquiry approach. Appreciative inquiry is a five-pronged process through which we will *Discover*, *Discern*, *Dream*, *Design*, and *Do*—all with an emphasis on our strengths.

Because it's adaptable for each individual, *The Gifted Journey* is for everyone and anyone, whether you're about to apply for colleges, you're just starting out in your career, you're a downsizing statistic, or you're simply unhappy with your current path in life and you need some directional input. Each of these situations can be a powerful catalyst to seeking change, and the five steps in *The Gifted Journey* can help you uncover your gifts and put them to work.

Additionally, *The Gifted Journey* can be used in a group setting—such as a high school class—to help students uncover their gifts and determine a positive path forward.

It's important that this journey be uniquely yours, which is why I will occasionally ask you to visit www.thegiftedjourney.com for supplementary materials that will help personalize and enrich your Gifted Journey experience. And please take a moment now to download *The Gifted Journey* MAP from *The Gifted Journey* site. It's free and will serve as your living, breathing companion as you move your way through each of the five steps in your journey.

Whenever you're ready, look to the next page, and let's begin!

CHAPTER ONE

Welcome to Your Gifted Journey

"Your soul knows the geography of your destiny. Your soul alone has the map of your future; therefore you can trust this indirect, oblique side of yourself. If you do, it will take you where you need to go, but more important it will teach you a kindness of rhythm in your journey."

—John O'Donohue, *Anam Cara: A Book of Celtic Wisdom*

Recognize What Brought You Here

Every journey, including yours, is unique, and because of that, I'd like you to pause a moment and think about why you are here and what you are hoping to gain from this process. Consider the following: How did your journey bring you to this point in time? What questions do you want answered? What clarity are you seeking? Below are a number of possible scenarios. As you read these, see if one fits your current situation.

Just Starting Out

If you're still pondering your path forward after high school, *The Gifted Journey* can help you make informed choices related to colleges and fields of study, or choices regarding a trade or other area of expertise to pursue out of high school.

Ready for the World

If your college days are nearing completion and you're looking toward your next step, this journey can help you think about the type of work that would be most fulfilling for you and how you could apply your knowledge, innate talents, and strengths right from the start.

Bored and Restless

Perhaps the path you've been on is no longer fulfilling, or maybe life itself feels more like "work" and is no longer fun or stimulating. Maybe a specific event triggered this epiphany, or maybe your indifference has grown gradually over time, and now you're numb to the potential of a truly rewarding life. Whatever the case, I ask that you open yourself up to the possibility that this process will not only shed light on why this has happened but also illuminate the possibilities going forward.

Others Determining or Directing Your Path

It could be that well-meaning friends, colleagues, parents, or other adults are, in some way, encouraging you to choose the path that *they* think is right for you. Perhaps it's the same path they chose for themselves, and they've achieved great success and are sure you will achieve the same results.

Conversely, they could be trying to help you avoid making the same mistakes they did to save you from the regret, frustration, and dissatisfaction that they have personally experienced. In fact, they may even dismiss your hopes and dreams by telling you to "Get real," or, "You would never be happy doing that job." Worse yet, "Trust me, I've been around, and I know what I'm talking about."

Deeper Longing

Another possible scenario is that you may be looking for something that speaks to a deeper longing. You may be wildly successful at your current career, but something's missing. Deep within your heart and soul you feel a powerful desire to do something else—something *more*—with your life.

Do any of these scenarios sound familiar? I know that one of them really rings true for me. During my first job right out of college, it was clear that others thought they knew what was best for me, and they tried to steer my career accordingly. I had been hired as a telemarketing rep selling residential telephones (the hard-wired kind) for a phone company. My first week was spent in sales training. I'll never forget the trainer. She walked into the room wearing a bright red suit, and not only did she make a statement with her clothing, she also had the teaching style to match. She was vibrant, funny, smart, and engaging. It was apparent that she was passionate about the subject matter and spoke from years of experience. She obviously loved what she was doing. I watched in fascination while she led us through that week—engaging us and holding our attention—and I realized that I was intrigued about this type of work. In fact, I was moved to find out more about this possible career path. After the training, I asked my manager for advice about finding a career in training. Her response was less than encouraging. It went something like this: "You don't want to do that kind of work. I've done it and it's really tough. You have to travel all the time and it's exhausting. Besides, you don't even have the experience or education to do that sort of work. You're better off doing what you are doing." And with that, she shot me a look that said, "Now get back to work!"

Have you ever had your hopes and dreams shut down inadvertently by some well-meaning person?

When there are outside influences directing our path, it can feel like we're "oozing" from role to role, or decision to decision. This lack of direction and control over our destiny can make us feel as though we never truly own our own lives. I've coached many individuals who felt like they had "settled" in their lives, and they can now appreciate how all the past advice, as well-meaning as it was, had led them there.

The Answer Awaits

As we prepare to begin your Gifted Journey, I want to emphasize that the goal is to move toward identifying your specific path. This process will require some reflection on what led you here. The intent is not to look back with regret. Instead, we will revisit the past with patience, compassion, and understanding. Your past experiences are important because this information will be the foundation you will use to inform your path forward.

Another goal of your Gifted Journey process is to increase self-awareness and clarity. The important thing to remember is that this process is different for everyone. Just as each of us is incredibly unique, so is this process. Some of the most common questions I've been asked over the years include, "What do you think I should do?" "Where do you think I should I go?" And, my favorite, "If you were me what would you do?" I remember, at times, feeling a bit guilty that I didn't have the perfect answer. Over the years, I've come to realize that, as much as I would LOVE to step onto your unique path or even use a crystal ball to predict your future, I unfortunately cannot. What I can offer you are my twenty-plus years of experience working with thousands of people at different stages in their lives and careers, walking them through specific steps in a process that led them to answers and a path forward. And now, I'm sharing this process with you. While the steps are the same for everyone, the outcome will be uniquely yours.

Your Life as a Kaleidoscope

I like to equate the Gifted Journey process to looking at life through a kaleidoscope. If you've ever looked through one and turned the cylinder, you saw an array of moving shapes and colors that together formed a pattern. Consider for a moment that those shapes and colors represent all the different facets of your life. Like a kaleidoscope filled with individual pieces, your life is made up of many individual experiences, which, over time, can reveal specific patterns. And, depending upon whether you point the kaleidoscope toward a bright window or toward a dark corner, the colors will look quite different. Your life and your experiences can also seem light or dark depending upon your perspective. Our goal is to recognize these shapes and colors and understand how they've contributed to the beauty in your journey so far. It's important to appreciate that every decision you've made up to this point has shaped you, creating a tapestry of colors and patterns that define your past.

Using Your Past to Inform Your Future

Why spend so much time studying your past experiences? Because you can use these experiences to inform your future choices. Later in this book, I will walk you through exercises that will help you uncover which paths from your past brought you joy and satisfaction, and which ones were less fulfilling. These exercises will provide you with a clear lens through which you can view any future opportunities. Going forward, you will be able to filter your choices and make decisions that are well informed and based on what you truly know about yourself.

Your Path Must Have a Heart

Remember, identifying your path forward is the ultimate goal of your Gifted Journey, and it's important for your chosen path to have a heart. Consider the following quote, which is one of my favorites:

"A path is only a path, and there is no affront, to oneself or to others, in dropping it if that is what your heart tells you . . . Look at every path closely and deliberately. Try it as many times as you think necessary. Then ask yourself alone, one question . . . Does this path have a heart? If it does, the path is good; if it doesn't it is of no use."

—Carlos Castaneda, *The Teachings of Don Juan: A Yaqui Way of Knowledge*

What does it mean for a path to have a heart? And how would you know? It is sometimes easier to recognize when a path does *not* have a heart because you may feel anxious, frustrated, drained, or stressed. A path without a heart can also trigger certain reactions like impatience, exhaustion, or depression, which, if left untreated, can lead to complications like high blood pressure, ulcers, headaches, chronic fatigue, or worse.

For three years I worked as a senior manager for a financial institution, and I was keenly aware that this job was not suited for me. More often than not, I dreaded going to work. I often woke up exhausted, still trying to recover from the prior day's stress. Some of the more frustrating and draining aspects of my job included creating daily financial spreadsheets, handling customer complaints, and managing individual performance problems. It wasn't uncommon for me to bring work home since there didn't seem to be enough hours in the day to accomplish everything. What I didn't realize was the toll my job was taking on my physical and mental health. At the beginning of my third year in the position, I started to experience severe headaches and stomach issues. I soon discovered that I had my first ulcer at the age of thirty. Shortly thereafter, I started having regular and unexplainable nose bleeds. These alarmed not only me but also my husband, who finally insisted I get these symptoms checked out by our physician. I will never forget this appointment. The doctor spent over an hour asking me a series of direct questions about what I did for a living, how much stress I was feeling, and how long my symptoms had been happening. During my responses, the past three years came flooding into full view. I saw, for the first time, the preponderance of days when my job had reduced me to tears. I saw the pain and frustration I'd tried to hide from everyone around me. The doctor listened patiently to all of my responses. Then, he silently reviewed my chart for what seemed an eternity. My epiphanies exploded like fireworks in my head and my eyes filled with tears. My doctor looked up at me and said, "I have your diagnosis and prescription. You need to quit your job because it is literally killing you."

Those three years—as miserable as they were—taught me a valuable lesson: it's hard to recognize how unhappy we are while we are in the midst of it. We become so consumed with simply getting everything accomplished that we're blind to the fact that our current circumstances are responsible for our fatigue, frustration, and depression. I realized later that, had my doctor not taken the time to ask me all of his pointed questions, I may never have come to the realization that my job was having such a negative impact on my body, mind, and spirit. My health could have continued its downward spiral and left me debilitated.

With all the pressure to earn a living, pay the mortgage, and provide for our families, I know it can be hard to accept that personal joy and happiness need to be parts of the equation. But after my appointment with my doctor, I knew beyond any shadow of a doubt that I needed to make significant changes in my life. I needed to figure out what I could do that would ultimately be less stressful and improve my chances of surviving in this world—those were my minimum requirements. What I later discovered, after years of doing my own exploration, is that in addition to survival, I could also experience joy and immense satisfaction doing work I absolutely loved.

To that point, back in the early nineties I shared this personal health story in one of my first career development workshops. A woman walked up to me during a break and exclaimed, "I've never thought about putting the word 'fun' with the word 'work'!"

So let's return to the question, what does a path with a heart look like? The heart can be described as your energy and passion for what you do, or the value you place on that work and your desire to want to do it. It could be that when others recognize your work it gives you a high level of satisfaction and a sense of appreciation. For me, when I began helping others on their career journeys, I felt extreme joy and satisfaction. No longer did I dread getting up and going to work. In essence, my path had a heart.

I believe that deep down in each of us is a yearning that speaks to us and inspires us to move in a certain direction. Once we find our path with a heart, we will know it.

This is why we must start the Gifted Journey process by looking at our past. We need to fully understand where we have been before we can know where to go.

Your Gifted Journey Tools

I'd like you to make use of the following valuable tools to help deepen and enrich your journey:

- *The Gifted Journey* **book** – The book you are holding is designed to be a journey in and of itself and is not meant to be a "quick read." My hope is that you will take your time and read each chapter thoroughly (maybe multiple times) and then spend some time reflecting after each step so that you can get the most out of this process.

- *The Gifted Journey* **website** – Occasionally, I will ask you to visit the website www.thegiftedjourney.com to download a digital exercise or to locate additional resources to support your process.

- *The Gifted Journey* **MAP** – You will find your personal copy of *The Gifted Journey* MAP at www.thegiftedjourney. com. The MAP, which stands for My Action Plan, will help you capture thoughts as you reflect at the end of each of the steps of the process and beyond.

Bring the Right People into Your Process

Along with your Gifted Journey tools, the *right* people are also critical to your process. I mentioned earlier that the wrong people can misdirect your path, but the right people can be a bridge to your future. Over the years I have learned that the Gifted Journey process is difficult to do on your own and in a vacuum. We need trusted individuals who are willing to go on this journey with us. They are like passengers in your car, sitting quietly and listening patiently as you share your thoughts. They can also be active passengers, pointing out road signs in your life that you may have missed. They can also confirm much of what you are learning about yourself through their own perspective and understanding. Having people along on the journey can make this a much more affirming and enjoyable experience. Just like my physician, whose questions and observations prompted me to change directions for the better, our trusted friends can offer insights that open our eyes to possibilities we may not have seen otherwise. These individuals will become integral parts of your journey, serving as sounding boards who reinforce much of what you're learning, and contributing their own perspectives when asked or needed.

Another key reason I've found outside perspectives so important to this process is that we can unknowingly discount the significance of our experiences or the impact we've made when looking inward. This can stem from a sense of humility or feeling unworthy of praise and affirmation. In essence, an outside perspective can give us the objectivity and affirmation that is critical for our own self-awareness. Also, when we can articulate out loud our own assessment of ourselves it will deepen the experience and the knowledge we gain. You will find that discussing your past experiences with someone you trust will help you build your self-confidence when it comes to choosing your future direction.

Stay Positive

The Gifted Journey process uses an appreciative inquiry approach, which keeps the focus on our strengths and gifts rather than on our weaknesses. This book isn't about "fixing" ourselves; it's about finding our truer selves and following the path we were meant to follow. Here's the definition of appreciative inquiry:

"[Appreciative Inquiry] deliberately seeks to discover people's exceptionality—their unique gifts, strengths, and qualities. It actively searches and recognizes people for their specialties—their essential contributions and achievements. And it is based on principles of equality of voice— everyone is asked to speak about their vision of the true, the good, and the possible. Appreciative Inquiry builds momentum and success because it believes in people. It really is an invitation to a positive revolution. Its goal is to discover in all human beings the exceptional and the essential. Its goal is to create organizations that are in full voice!"[1]

There is much information emerging these days on the validity of identifying and nurturing strengths as opposed to fixing weaknesses, and we owe a world of gratitude to pioneers in the arena of positive psychology such as Donald Clifton, who is considered the "Father of Positive Psychology." Early in Dr. Clifton's research, he was interested in looking at the positive side of human nature as opposed to the negative. In fact, he started by asking one simple question: "What will happen when we think about what is right with people rather than fixating on what is wrong with them?" Think about how profound that question is and how it challenges conventional wisdom.

See Your Life in 5-D

Your Gifted Journey will follow five distinct steps: *Discover*, *Discern*, *Dream*, *Design*, and *Do*. I like to think of the process as seeing your life through 5-D glasses.

We will devote a full chapter to each of the five steps in your Gifted Journey and walk through them together in greater detail. But for now, here's a brief explanation of each.

Discover. How well do you really understand the impact and value of your personal gifts, talents, and strengths? If you have enjoyed most of your past work experiences, you may already have a solid understanding of where your talents can contribute within an organization. However, if you are like many who've come through my coaching sessions, this may be the first time you've looked at yourself this closely. Your assessment of yourself forms the foundation of your Gifted Journey, which is why it's step one. There are many ways in which we can assess who we are and why. What is most important is to look at this self-assessment information through an objective mindset. By doing so, you will have the most accurate information and the best language to describe who you are. As part of the *Discover* step, we will look at a number of ways to gather this vital information. Specifically, we will assess the following:

- **Discover Exercise 1: Your Early Years to Present Day** – In this exercise, we will look at your childhood and early adult experiences to identify those that were enjoyable versus those that were not. This is how we will start to identify some of your innate talents and motivations.

- **Discover Exercise 2: Your Values** – In this exercise, we will assess your core values. Your values are like your North Star—they direct and guide your actions. When our values are aligned with how we live our lives and how we do our work, we are happy and satisfied; when they are not we can be frustrated and unhappy.

- **Discover Exercise 3: A Good Day vs. Bad Day** – This exercise gives clarity to those activities and experiences that are most enjoyable to us. This will help us articulate why certain environments drain us while others excite and energize us.

- **Discover Exercise 4: Illustrate Your Best Day** – Here you will illustrate what a "great day" looks like—specifically, what you are doing, who you are doing it with, and what impact you are making. This exercise helps bring your strengths to life.

- **Discover Exercise 5: Your Motivated Skills and Abilities** – This exercise will help you articulate and deepen your understanding of your motivated skills and abilities—those that make you feel strong and confident and those skills you love to use and that energize you. We will call these motivated skills and abilities your *strengths*. This exercise will also highlight experiences that leave you feeling drained and frustrated, which will help us pinpoint areas we will refer to as your *weaknesses.*

- **Discover Exercise 6: Assess Your Innate Talents** – This exercise uses the CliftonStrengths assessment and will help you identify signature talent themes. These talent themes are our unique and natural way of thinking, feeling, and behaving. This assessment can help us understand the "why" of our strengths. When productively applied, our talents can help us reach high levels of expertise in areas that we really enjoy.

- **Discover Exercise 7: How Do Others See Me?** – In this exercise, you will ask others to assess your top motivated skills and strengths. This exercise will give you a more well-rounded assessment of your strengths and their impact.

Discern. We will begin the second step of *The Gifted Journey* by looking in a rearview mirror to see where you've been, what you've recently missed, and what is fast approaching. The goal of the *Discern* step is to apply what you've learned about your past to help define your path forward.

We will look back and reflect on specific, pivotal events in your life to help you understand who you are and what has impacted and defined your life to this point. We will then compare those experiences with the information gained from the exercises in step one (*Discover*) to uncover any patterns and themes as they relate to your personal and professional success and satisfaction. We need a thorough understanding of our past before we can create a path to a more rewarding future.

The *Discern* phase can be likened to preparing a carefully crafted resume: you don't want to include *everything* you've ever done. You want to analyze your past experiences and include only those you want to take with you going forward.

To help you identify the skills and experiences that have the most value and that bring you the most joy, we'll work through the following exercises:

- **Discern Exercise 1: What am I Learning About Myself?** – In this exercise, you will review all the information you have gathered about yourself through the exercises and assessments and walk through a process to reflect, evaluate, and summarize the themes that surface.

- **Discern Exercise 2: What Have I Learned About Myself from Others?** – In this exercise, you will also consider the feedback you've received from your trusted advisers—those people who know you well and can see your strengths and weaknesses from an objective perspective. This can help reaffirm what you know about yourself and, in some cases, shine a light on areas you may never have considered or thought of before.

- **Discern Exercise 3: What Recurring Themes are Emerging?** – In this exercise, you will document all of the recurring themes that are coming from your own assessments as well as from the feedback and input from others.

- **Discern Exercise 4: What, if Anything, Am I Missing?** – In this exercise, you will note anything you may be missing or that requires further follow-up. This may include interviews with trusted friends and family members who can help confirm the themes you are seeing or close gaps in your understanding of yourself and your experiences.

- **Discern Exercise 5: Continue to Discern as You Move Forward** – In this exercise, we will cover the practice of ongoing discernment as a way to increase your mindfulness of this process and your journey.

Dream. In step three, you will take all that you have learned about yourself from *Discover* and *Discern* and look toward the future. This is not an "action" step, but rather, a time to dream about all the possibilities and paths going forward.

I like to compare this step to dreaming about the perfect vacation. Where would you love to go and why? Would there be palm trees or ice-capped mountains? Nonstop walking tours through ancient ruins or relaxing days at sea? Or a little of all of the above? How would you feel in your ideal environment? What sorts of activities would you engage in to bring you joy?

Like a dream vacation, the third step in your Gifted Journey is to create a vision of the perfect environment for you. As you can imagine, this is a critical step. Time spent thinking about your ideal future and painting a detailed picture in your mind can truly help your dream manifest itself in reality. I've known people who've wanted to gloss over this step, jump right in, and apply assessment data to their current environments. Perhaps they've had their dreams censored or filtered in the past, or they still lack a clear path going forward. But these reasons are exactly why more time—not less time—should be spent in the *Dream* step of *The Gifted Journey*.

Again, *Dream* is where other people can be great resources. However, their role in this step will be to listen closely without critiquing. This is not about the likelihood of your dreams becoming reality; this is about the value of the process itself. You want to surround yourself with friends, colleagues, mentors, and/or a coach who can actively listen to your dreams and ask you the right questions to help you bring your visions into focus.

So, what would it look like if you were using your talents and strengths every day? We'll use the following exercises to get you started:

- **Dream Exercise 1: Let Your Mind Explore** – In this exercise, you will spend reflective time creating images in your mind. The purpose of this exercise is to let your mind go beyond what may be "real" and to imagine an ideal environment where you are actively engaged in activities and situations where you feel strong, competent, and happy.

- **Dream Exercise 2: Determine Your Focus** – In this exercise, you will use the images you created in Dream Exercise 1 to help you define your overall focus for your future. You will do this by answering a series of questions meant to help you clarify your path forward.

- **Dream Exercise 3: Create a Personal Vision Statement** – Making important decisions without a vision statement is like planning a trip without a destination. In this exercise, you will create your Personal Vision Statement in which you will articulate what you hope will be the end result of all your hard work, all your careful planning, and all the choices you made that led you down the right path. This is your ultimate destination and will give your path direction.

- **Dream Exercise 4: Continue to Dream all the way to Self-Actualization** – In this exercise, you will increase your chances of living your vision by practicing a powerful self-actualization technique. You will intentionally plant your vision in your mind so that the reality of your dream starts to manifest in your activities and choices.

Design. In the fourth step, we will take everything we've gathered so far and assemble all the pieces to create the beginning of an action plan to help direct you on your path forward. This is where you will start to think about a tangible goal for yourself and look for practical activities that will move you forward. For instance, if you are "stuck" in your current role, what would a goal look like for you? Perhaps it would be to broaden your experience or to learn more about a field that interests you. It may be that you love what you do but you want a different environment to do it in. It may be that you are just starting out and you want to make sure you are emphasizing your strengths and motivated skills so that opportunities that align with your goal are the ones that surface for you. The key of *Design* is to establish a goal and then look for ways to leverage your talents and strengths so that you can achieve it. To help you draft your plan, we will work through the following exercises:

- **Design Exercise 1: Create Your Goal** – A clearly stated goal can help drive your plan of action. Your goal can be broken into multiple parts and timeframes. For instance, you may have an immediate need to find a more fulfilling role, so in the short term, you may want to focus on the here and now. You may also have a longer-term, ultimate goal that spans the next one to five years.

In this exercise, you will articulate your goal in great detail, breaking it down into manageable parts that you can achieve in the next six months, two years, and five years. Your milestones could be anything from pursuing your first job in your dream career to changing into a role that will use your strengths and talents in a more productive way. You could also look for ways to enhance your current role; in other words, "bloom where you are planted."

- **Design Exercise 2: Develop SMART Objectives to Reach Your Goal** – Having clear objectives gives you clarity on how you will achieve your goal. Not only should they be clear, they should also be SMART: Specific, Measurable, Attainable, Relevant, and Timely. Identifying your objectives in this way will increase your likelihood of success.

- **Design Exercise 3: Create Your Own Personal Board of Directors** – These are the people who you have chosen to be integral parts of your journey. Typically, these individuals are people you trust and can provide guidance, coaching, encouragement, and support as part of your overall plan.

Do. This is the *action* part of the plan—the commitment to take that next step in your journey and move one step closer toward your goal. By now, the first four steps of the process should be moving you toward a logical path, and in this fifth and final step, we will put our assessments, introspection, dreams, and designs into action!

- **Do Exercise 1: Connect with Others** – In this exercise, you will set up one coffee or lunch date with a colleague, mentor, coach, or a member of your personal board of directors each week.

- **Do Exercise 2: Revisit and Update Your MAP** – In this exercise, you will make the commitment to actively review your MAP at regularly scheduled intervals, such as once a month, to reaffirm your goals, capture your accomplishments, and note your progress.

- **Do Exercise 3: Create a Plan to be a Continuous Learner** – In this exercise, you will identify the skills, knowledge, and experiences that you need to further develop the abilities that align with your chosen path.

- **Do Exercise 4: Reflect and Record Your Daily Experiences** – In this exercise, using a series of questions, you will be encouraged to reflect and record your daily experiences as a way to keep your journey alive and relevant.

Summary

Your Gifted Journey is Both a Process and a Destination

Did you ever take a family vacation or go camping with friends? Remember that sense of excitement when you loaded up the car and prepared yourself to embark on a new adventure? I remember taking the annual family vacation to Reno with my grandparents. I can still recall the feeling of excitement as we loaded up the car and pulled out of the driveway. Although the destination was the same every year, the experiences along the way could be quite different. My grandparents loved playing the "alphabet game" where we had to find words that started with each letter of the alphabet in the proper order. We could use road signs, billboards, restaurants—virtually anything. Not only was it fun, but it also made us look out the windows and take note of our surroundings. Year after year, I spotted interesting sights that were either new or that I had overlooked in the past.

That is how I hope your Gifted Journey feels to you. I hope you're excited about what you will see, what you will learn, and what may change you forever. Although it's tempting to focus on the destination, I encourage you to take careful note of the road signs along the way. I will also encourage you to stop and stay a bit where there are places of interest. And, just like my family's annual trip to Reno, many sights will be familiar to you, and many will be new. I encourage you to view all of your experiences through a clear lens and with a sense of discovery. It is only through this newfound heightened awareness that we can learn more about our past and anticipate how it may inform our future.

CHAPTER TWO

Step One: Discover

*"Our deepest fear is not that we are inadequate. Our deepest fear is
that we are powerful beyond measure."*

— Marianne Williamson

Who Am I?

To understand the power of our truest self, we must first learn
everything we can about ourselves. In step one, *Discover*, we will
ponder one of life's greatest questions: Who am I?

As I mentioned earlier, it took a physician to tell me I was on the
wrong path. But how was I supposed to find the right one? I tried
asking myself how I ended up where I did and what I really wanted
to do, but back in the early 1980s, there weren't a lot of career
development resources. One colleague pointed me in the direction of "career outplacement," which I soon discovered were firms
that helped those who had been laid off. Although outplacement
services weren't exactly what I was seeking, the idea of outplacement as a career in and of itself piqued my interest. I scheduled
informational interviews with several companies to learn as much
as I could about outplacement. To my immense joy, I was offered
a contract position with the largest global outplacement firm at
that time and was given the gift of learning a career development
process. Twenty years later, I am still invested in the process even
as it has evolved over time.

After working with many clients who had spent years in their careers, I can appreciate how daunting it can be when trying to answer the question, Who am I? My guess is that you've had many experiences both inside and outside of the workplace that have shaped you in unique ways. And yet, it can be difficult to dissect those experiences, especially those that happened years ago and have now become part of a fuzzy past. We need to go back and look closely at some of those experiences because they can become clues to our future.

Speaking of clues, one way to approach this step is to think of yourself as an archaeologist who is interested in uncovering articles from your past. You will look at these articles for what they are. I'm going to encourage you to take your time with this process and do this at your own pace. *The Gifted Journey* MAP is the ideal place to capture your thoughts as you reflect on these exercises. Later in the second step of *The Gifted Journey*, which is *Discern*, I will encourage you to reflect a bit deeper on key experiences to determine their meaning and impact.

A Journey Back in Time

Looking back on your early years will help shed some light on your preferences and your interests. Early on, our external and internal experiences plant seeds that grow and shape how we ultimately see the world. Our brains are highly adept at assembling patterns and themes from our experiences, and these emerging patterns will guide us toward certain situations. For instance, were you the one who starred in the school play or were you more interested in building the sets? Maybe you were drawn to sports, or dancing, or art, or reading, or writing. Where did you experience joy and fun? The key is that even as children, we gravitate toward and respond to different things at different times. Here is where we start to develop interests, talents, and passions. Some of your interests may have been very different from those of your siblings or friends. These are the early signs of your unique being. Recognizing these connections is a powerful first step in beginning your Gifted Journey.

Discover Exercise 1: Your Early Years to Present Day

In this exercise, take some time to answer the following questions about your school years and (if applicable) work experiences. Please note that if answers don't immediately come to you, that's OK! Simply move on to the next question. I would, however, suggest that you let these questions float around in your mind. You may reach out to those who know you well and see if they can help fill in some of the blanks.

Early childhood through grammar school

1. What were some of your earliest positive memories? What was it that made them so positive?

_____

_____

_____

_____

_____

2. As a young child, how would your parents, caregivers, siblings, and/or friends describe you?

_____

_____

_____

_____

_____

3. What did you enjoy doing as a young child? (playing games, entertaining others, reading books, solving puzzles, laughing with friends, competing in sports)

_____

_____

_____

_____

_____

_____

4. What types of books did you enjoy reading or what types of stories did you enjoy most? (fiction, nonfiction, history, biographies, entertainment)

_____

_____

_____

_____

_____

_____

5. What were your favorite subjects in grammar school?

_____

_____

_____

_____

_____

6. What subjects were more difficult for you and why?

_____

_____

_____

_____

_____

_____

Junior high through high school

1. What subjects did you most enjoy and which did you excel in?

_____

_____

_____

_____

_____

_____

2. What extracurricular activities (social groups, clubs, sports, leadership) did you participate in? And what did you enjoy most about these activities?

_____

_____

_____

_____

_____

_____

Undergraduate and graduate school (if applicable)

1. What degree did you pursue and why? What was most satisfying about that subject?

_____

_____

_____

_____

_____

_____

2. What positive experiences stand out?

_____

_____

_____

_____

_____

_____

Professional/work experiences

1. What was your first job? What were your responsibilities? What was most interesting about that job? What parts did you like? What parts did you dislike?

_____

_____

_____

_____

_____

2. What other types of jobs have you had? What was most satisfying about each of these roles?

_____

_____

_____

_____

_____

_____

3. What do you do today? What is most satisfying about your
   current role?

_____

_____

_____

_____

_____

_____

Themes and Patterns Emerge

As you reflect on your answers to these questions, are you spotting
any themes or patterns? This is not a coincidence. These are the
seeds that were planted early on. Some are part of your unique and
innate nature, and some have been formed through your experiences in school, work, and life. Some may have been formed
through input from the people in your life, such as your parents,
relatives, teachers, and others.

Let's take a closer look at some of these seeds and when they were planted.

Discover Exercise 2: Your Values

In the midst of any helpful self-assessment process you should see patterns emerging that come from the core of who you really are. But what, exactly, drove the creation of these patterns? One word: values. Our values are foundational (and fundamental) to our joy and satisfaction, not to mention our purpose and meaning. The online *Business Dictionary* defines values as "important and lasting beliefs or ideals shared by the members of a culture about what is good or bad and desirable or undesirable. Values have major influence on a person's behavior and attitude and serve as broad guidelines in all situations."[2]

Our values shape our attitudes, our decisions, and the construct of how we live our lives. If your actions and behaviors align with your values, your life will be satisfying; if not, you will experience boredom, restlessness, anxiety, fear, and anger. Our values are critical to our happiness and sense of well-being. In fact, renowned psychologist Abraham Maslow believed that our values were at the heart of our motivational system.

Values that grow from the "core of who you are" are enduring and may stay with you throughout your life. Some will change based upon your circumstances.

The following values assessment will help you determine your top values.

Values assessment

Review and reflect on the topics below and select the words that best align with your values. There is no limit to the number you can select.

I value a career oriented toward:	I value a work culture that provides:	In work relationships I value:	My core intrinsic values are:
❏ Challenge	❏ Flexibility	❏ Teamwork	❏ Integrity
❏ Leading others	❏ Deadline pressure	❏ Trust	❏ Status
❏ Competence	❏ Surroundings	❏ Cultural identity	❏ Prestige
❏ Mastery	❏ Time freedom	❏ Caring	❏ Achievement
❏ Risk	❏ Security	❏ Competition	❏ Respect
❏ Leading edge	❏ High earnings	❏ Cooperation	❏ Responsibility
❏ Data and details	❏ Action-oriented	❏ Diversity	❏ Power
❏ Social activism	❏ Structure	❏ Collaboration	❏ Influence
❏ Learning	❏ Relaxed pace	❏ Humor	❏ Appreciation
❏ Excellence	❏ Casual	❏ Harmony	❏ Helping
❏ Focus	❏ Quiet	❏ Autonomy	❏ Belonging
❏ Creativity	❏ Organized	❏ Recognition	❏ Community
❏ Variety	❏ Excitement	❏ Support	❏ Equality
❏ Growth	❏ Pressure	❏ Open communication	❏ Independence
❏ Knowledge	❏ Predictability	❏ People contact	❏ Contributing
❏ Control	❏ Location	❏ Independence	❏ Service
❏ Adventure	❏ Public contact	❏ Fun	❏ Authenticity
❏ Helping	❏ Comfortable income		❏ Commitment
❏ Initiating			❏ Balance
			❏ Honesty
			❏ Having an impact
			❏ Fairness

Select your top 10 values

To help you identify your top values, pick your top ten values from those you've checked. This doesn't mean that the other values you initially checked are not important. Narrowing your choices down to ten will help you determine your *core* values. Pay close attention to your inner dialogue as you make choices. Your process will reveal interesting truths about yourself.

After you select what you feel best represents your top ten values, write them below.

1. _____   6. _____

2. _____   7. _____

3. _____   8. _____

4. _____   9. _____

5. _____   10. _____

Select your top 5 values

Now we'll refine your list once more. Choose five of your top ten values and record them in the chart below, along with a brief explanation of how you would define that value for yourself.

My Top 5 Values	Description
1.	
2.	
3.	
4.	
5.	

(Note: There are a number of values instruments available. This exercise is designed to get you started down this path.)

Questions to ponder:

- How easy or difficult was it to choose your top ten values?

- How easy or difficult was it to narrow it down to your top five?

- As you look at those top five, how do they relate to your experiences in life leading up to today?

- How have your values shaped the person you are today?

- How have your values played a part in the directions you've chosen leading up to today?

- When have your values been in conflict? What impact did that have on you?

- Some values can change over time. Which would you consider nonnegotiable, enduring values?

Discover Exercise 3: A Good Day vs. Bad Day

This next exercise is one that I've used in my career development work for more than twenty years. It is a simple yet revealing exercise for many.

In this exercise, you will reflect on Good Day and Bad Day experiences that occurred within a relatively short span of time. I find it most helpful (and more accurate) to look to your recent past. You could choose one week, two weeks, or an entire month if your memory serves you. The key here is to choose a specific interval for which you can still recall in detail your activities, tasks, conversations, projects, and assignments.

In the Good Day column, capture all of the things that you really enjoyed down to the smallest detail. Did you work on a problem you were able to solve? Did you participate in a brainstorming session that left you energized? Did you come up with a new idea that everyone seemed excited about? Did you complete an assignment that you had committed to? Did you help resolve a conflict between other people? List as many things as you can on the positive side of the page.

On the Bad Day side, jot down all of those things that drained you or frustrated you. A project that was difficult to complete? An unresolved conflict with a co-worker? A meeting that reached no conclusion or outcome? Lack of appreciation from your boss or co-workers? Ideas that were dismissed or criticized?

Once you've written down all the positives and negatives you can remember for the timeframe that you've chosen, you can move on to the next exercise.

Good Day	Bad Day

Discover Exercise 4: Illustrate Your Best Day

As you are thinking about your Good Day vs. Bad Day exercise, I'd like you to consider your very best day. Think about a day when you were energized and happy, and it felt as if everything was in sync and, as a result, time flew by.

In this exercise, while not necessary, I would strongly encourage you to grab some colored pencils or markers and illustrate your BEST day. Think about a day when you were doing what you loved, where you felt strong and confident, and where perhaps you even received some positive recognition. The important thing is to capture what you were doing, who you were doing it with (if anyone), and the environment you were in.

The first time I did this exercise I drew a picture of myself standing in front of a room with people sitting at round tables engaged in lively discussion. I was in the front of the room facilitating the experience. It looked something like this:

By the way, this exercise has nothing to do with artistic talent, and stick figures are more than acceptable!

YOUR BEST DAY!

I use this exercise because it reinforces and affirms what we already know about ourselves. It brings to the forefront of our consciousness a tangible image of us at our best. It reminds us that we have already had experiences involving our innate talents and emerging strengths.

Discover Exercise 5: Your Motivated Skills and Abilities

Next, we are going to bring that picture of a perfect day to life by adding descriptive language to it. The importance of this exercise is to provide a vocabulary or language to describe what you do well so that you can easily articulate it to others.

Look through the sample list of possible activities and check off those that best describe your finest work and those that bring you great joy and satisfaction.

- ❑ Solving complex problems
- ❑ Building relationships
- ❑ Brainstorming ideas and solutions
- ❑ Creating a plan
- ❑ Collaborating with different individuals
- ❑ Mentoring or coaching others
- ❑ Analyzing data
- ❑ Creating spreadsheets
- ❑ Leading small groups
- ❑ Presenting to others
- ❑ Training on technical topics
- ❑ Training on development topics
- ❑ Facilitating meetings
- ❑ Moving people into action
- ❑ Building complex systems
- ❑ Resolving conflict
- ❑ Organizing information
- ❑ Working on creative projects
- ❑ Selling ideas or solutions
- ❑ Getting things done

What's missing? What other activities would you add to this list?

1. _____

2. _____

3. _____

4. _____

5. _____

Later, you will find this page of activities to be useful in many circumstances. For instance, you can use this to fill out a college application. It can also be used when creating a resume, professional bio, or social media page. It can also be used when interviewing for a position, or as part of a performance plan or review.

Discover Exercise 6: Assess Your Innate Talents

Think of your talents as the seeds that were planted early in your life. These innate talents affect how we think, feel, and behave, and become the foundation of our strengths. Dr. Donald Clifton, an educational psychologist, and his team conducted more than forty years of research on innate talent and developed the Clifton StrengthsFinder assessment (currently known as CliftonStrengths) in the 1990s. The assessment measures your natural talent within thirty-four themes to help you better understand your strengths when it comes to building relationships, strategic thinking, executing plans, and influencing others. The online assessment consists of nearly two hundred questions and produces a customized report defining what it calls your Signature Themes. It will provide you with specific actions you can take based on best practices. As of this book's writing, nearly nineteen million people have taken the CliftonStrengths assessment, and it is used extensively in education, nonprofit, and corporate environments.

Taking the CliftonStrengths assessment

You can locate and complete the CliftonStrengths assessment at www.gallupstrengthscenter.com. Please note that there is a charge for this assessment. It is not a requirement of your Gifted Journey process, but I believe it can provide valuable insight into your talents and potential strengths.

If you choose to complete the assessment, please print out one of your available reports. I personally like the "Insight Action Planning Guide" as it provides you with a customized definition of each of your top five talent themes.

Once you have your report in hand, thoroughly read and digest each definition of your top five talent themes. It is helpful to highlight or underline key words or phrases that best describe you. You can capture these steps here:

Top 5 talent themes	Key words or phrases that best describe you	Recent situation in which you applied the talents from this theme
1.		
2.		
3.		

4.		
5.		

At this point, you may want to consider connecting with a certified Gallup strengths coach. On our Gifted Journey website we have identified certified and trained coaches that you can reach out to who support the entire Gifted Journey process. Or you can go directly to the directory of coaches on the Gallup site at https://www.gallupstrengthscenter.com/ coach/en-us/directory/.

Talents and Strengths: How They Work Together to Inform Your Future

First, let's look at definitions of talent and strength. Gallup's definitions are as follows:

Talent: A natural, recurring pattern of thoughts, feelings, or behaviors that can be productively applied

Strength: A near-perfect performance in an activity you enjoy

So how do you link a talent to a strength? This is where you add experience, skills, and knowledge to the equation. It looks like this:

Talent x (Experience + Skills + Knowledge) = Strength

Your experience, (motivated) skills, and knowledge are where you invest time and energy. The key is looking at all you've learned and acquired in skills and knowledge and seeing where those skills and knowledge grew into strengths. Then, you need to look at your talents and see the role they played in converting those skills into strengths.

A simplified equation looks like this:

Talent x Investment = Strength

You may notice that, based on the order in which we've completed the previous exercises, we are now reverse engineering the formula:

Strengths = Investment x Talent

In Discover Exercise 1, we started by looking at what you already knew about yourself and your strengths—those areas of your life where you excel and feel the greatest sense of joy and satisfaction.

In Discover Exercises 3, 4, 5, and 6 we looked at which motivated skills, abilities, and knowledge are at play when you are operating from a strength. Then, we made the connection to your innate talents—the true *WHY* you are good at certain things.

Take, for instance, a person with exceptional presentation skills. If you've ever been in the presence of a great teacher or presenter, you probably noticed their ability to captivate an audience and target the information appropriately. They know just the right amount of detail to cover, how to use relevant stories and analogies, and how to artfully handle questions in a way that leaves the audience feeling satisfied with the answers.

How does one become highly efficient and even an expert at presenting information? Some would say that it requires "natural" talent. While certain folks may have innate talent, I truly believe (as a speech coach for years) that anyone can learn to be an effective presenter if they can just find their unique voice. Their voice is not only their expert knowledge but also their unique style and innate talent. When someone taps into their innate talent and adds their experience and expertise, along with some skill development, they can see their strength shine.

Discover Exercise 7: How Do Others See You?

One of the common reactions I hear once people look at their CliftonStrengths assessment is, "I'm not sure all of these talents are me." Or, "I thought other talents would be closer to the top of my list." This is where an outside perspective can be very helpful.

Whether or not you took the CliftonStrengths assessment, I believe you will find great value in this exercise. I'd like you to do the following exercise yourself as well as distribute it to about seven people you trust and who know you well. You can download a digital version of this exercise from www.thegiftedjourney.com so you can email it easily.

Dear _____ ,

In an effort to create a plan for my future, I would like to gain your perspective on my talents and strengths to better inform and confirm my path forward. Your insights will help me understand how others see my unique abilities. If you are willing, please answer the following questions. Please let me know once you have completed it. I would like to schedule thirty minutes to review it with you. Thank you.

Please look over the list of words below and circle all those that describe me:

Adaptable	Caring
Ambitious	Courageous
Compassionate	Spiritual
Considerate	Thorough
Courteous	Humorous
Creative	Sensible
Determined	Inspiring
Focused	Impartial
Intuitive	Reliable
Passionate	Inventive
Rational	Sincere
Sympathetic	Witty
Thoughtful	Generous
Warm	Affectionate

1. Based on the words you circled, where do you see my specific talents and strengths?

_____

_____

_____

_____

_____

_____

2. Can you give me one or two specific examples (activities, situations) of where you've seen my strengths?

_____

_____

_____

_____

_____

3. What impact have those activities or situations had on you or on others?

_____

_____

_____

_____

_____

Summary

As we wrap up *Discover*, my hope is that you have gained some new perspective on who you are and where you are in your journey so far. Take a moment to go to your MAP and answer the following questions (you can download the MAP at www.thegiftedjourney. com):

- What did I affirm about myself through each of the exercises?
- What did I learn about myself that was new?
- What did I learn from others that was surprising? What was affirming?

In the next step, *Discern*, we will reflect on all your past experiences and assessment information and start to discern which parts of your past are worth taking with you into the future.

CHAPTER THREE

Step Two: Discern

"Everything in your life is a reflection of a choice you have made. If you want a different result, make a different choice."

—Anonymous

Take Note of What You're Learning About Yourself

In our second step, *Discern*, we are going to reflect on all the information you have gathered in step one. The goal is to bring more clarity to what you are learning about yourself and what others have shared with you.

What does it mean to discern? For our purposes, discernment means reflecting upon past experiences in a highly objective way and then evaluating the meaning of these experiences. The goal at this point in *The Gifted Journey* is to form connections between your positive and negative life experiences and the assessments you have completed so far. Using this information, you are now going to look for themes that define who you are.

Earlier in Chapter One we talked about the importance of bringing people along as part of your process. Here is where finding the right people becomes really important. The *Discern* step can be difficult to complete effectively on your own and with only your individual reflection and interpretation. The reason this is difficult for many is because we tend to downplay the significance of our past, our accomplishments, our joy, and our happiness, especially if we are currently in a more difficult place in our journey. We tend to forget those times of joy and satisfaction if the current path is dissatisfying or stress-filled. This is where an outside perspective can be highly beneficial. Discussing your past experiences and assessments with trusted friends and colleagues who know you well can be illuminating and give you an even deeper level of understanding.

For instance, early on in Chapter One I shared the story of my first job out of college. I was working as a telemarketing representative at a phone company, and during an employee training session I caught a glimpse of what I really wanted to do when a vibrant facilitator in a striking red suit provided our sales training. My manager at that time did not encourage me to pursue my newfound interest (although there would later be a glimmer of hope within this organization, and there's more on that story in my Afterword). A few years later, through a downsizing, I was forced to look for another job, and that's when I landed at the financial institution where I experienced great stress and eventually sought medical attention. Even though my past had shown me the potential of a great path forward, I ended up in a role that was not suited for my strengths. During my time at the bank, I didn't even realize how far off the path I had gone, and I certainly didn't have the tools to know how to course correct. It took a doctor's pointed questions to get me to really reflect on my past and make me realize I had taken a wrong turn. I'm not sure I would have had the objectivity at the time to realize that a significant change was needed. Soon after my doctor's "diagnosis," I also sought out a wonderful former manager and a few friends who knew me well. I spent hours talking to them and seeking their insights into my past to see where I'd overlooked opportunities to do what I really loved. I was then reminded of the lady in the red suit, and I remembered how grateful I was for that sales training experience and how I'd envisioned a future for myself in which I was doing this type of training and coaching work for others. I started to feel that sense of excitement and optimism again. I had found my path!

In addition to someone who knows you well, you may also want the help of a mentor or coach. The main quality you want to look for in a mentor is the ability to actively listen and respond with reflective questions that will encourage you to look deeper into your experiences and help you continue to connect the dots.

The Value of an Objective Perspective

Let's take this one step further. Have you ever watched yourself on video? I remember seeing myself on camera for the first time. I was giving a presentation, and my initial reaction to watching the video was, "Do I really sound like that?" And, "Is that really me?" I also noticed a few distracting behaviors like speaking too quickly and rocking back and forth. Fortunately, I found a great speech coach who patiently listened to my initial critique and helped me appreciate the positive qualities that I was displaying. It was that objective viewpoint that helped me step outside of my own critical self-assessment and see myself from the audience's perspective.

Now as a presentation skills coach myself, I can truly empathize with people who dread public speaking. I also understand that our internal self-critics are just waiting for an opportunity to tell us how silly or uncomfortable we look.

This is why it's so helpful to have a coach who can balance your perspective and help you see your experiences from an external point of view. A trusted friend, coach, or mentor can soften that internal criticism while helping you shift your focus toward your talents and strengths. An objective perspective can affirm (validate) what you may already know about yourself, provide confirmation (reassurance), and open your eyes to skills that you weren't aware of. These objective observations will add to your overall understanding of how you are perceived.

Discern Exercise 1: What am I Learning About Myself?

Let's begin by reflecting on the following questions:

1. Looking back through the exercises in *Discover*, what themes seem to be emerging about who I am and what I do best?

_____

_____

_____

_____

_____

2. How closely have my top values aligned with my experiences in school, work, and life?

_____

_____

_____

_____

_____

3. What are my motivated skills and talents and how have they influenced my life choices and experiences?

_____

_____

_____

_____

_____

4. What lessons have I learned about myself that will help me as I move forward?

_____

_____

_____

_____

_____

_____

5. Looking back, where did I feel a sense of joy and satisfaction— that feeling that I was on the right path?

_____

_____

_____

_____

_____

_____

This particular exercise helped me greatly when I started to look closely at my past experiences. It was during this reflection that I made some key discoveries about my path. When I started to evaluate both my experiences and my feelings in different circumstances, I discovered where I was most happy and content. It was always when I was teaching, training, or coaching others. During those times, I felt like I was on the right path.

Lack of Discernment Can Lead You Astray

Spending time in the _Discern_ step is critical because it's very easy to be led astray by outside influences. As an example, in my career I have been encouraged to leave my training and coaching roles for management opportunities. The first time I was asked it was very flattering so I took the position. I learned soon after that there are many aspects of leading people that can be very rewarding, and I also learned that, for me, a management role did not fully play to my strengths and talents. I found myself longing to get back to the joy and satisfaction of training and coaching. Eventually, I made the transition back into the work I loved. However, because I hadn't taken the time to discern my past experiences, I ended up going into management two more times in my life. Each time I moved into a leadership role, I quickly realized that I had gone down the wrong path. It wasn't until later, and through this discernment process, that I learned once and for all that my joy would always lie in training and coaching. So I founded my own training company, and twenty years later I still feel I'm on the right path.

Discern Exercise 2: What Have I Learned About Myself from Others?

In this exercise, you are going to look at the insights you have gained from the questionnaire you shared with others in Discover Exercise 7.

1. What specific motivated skills and talents did they highlight that affirm and confirm what I already know about myself?

---

2. What skills and talents did they see in me that I had never recognized or noticed about myself?

_____

_____

_____

_____

_____

_____

Discern Exercise 3: What Recurring Themes are Emerging?

In this exercise, take time to consider any recurring themes that are popping up. For instance, based on your assessments and all of your past experiences as well as what you are hearing from others, are there certain strengths that are always present? For instance, are you someone people can count on to follow through on action items? Are you someone who people naturally gravitate toward for counsel or a listening ear? Are you someone who knows how to organize an event so that everyone feels welcomed and included? Are you someone who has a keen attention to detail? Take some time now to go back over your assessments and interviews and see if certain themes bubble to the surface.

Themes

_____

_____

_____

_____

_____

_____

Discern Exercise 4: What, if Anything, Am I Missing?

In this exercise, note anything that you need to clarify. For instance, do you need to schedule a conversation with someone who gave you feedback so you can gain more insight into their comments around your strengths and talents?

1. What information do I need to clarify from my assessments?

_____

_____

_____

_____

_____

_____

2. What information do I need to clarify from those I interviewed?

_____

_____

_____

_____

_____

_____

Discern Exercise 5: Continue to Discern Going Forward

Reflection and evaluation can be true gifts during the *Discern* phase and in daily practice. Spend time at the end of each day answering these questions:

- What did I do today that I really enjoyed?
- What were the high points of this day?
- What did I accomplish?

- Where did I feel energized?
- Where did I feel drained and frustrated?

To really answer these questions thoroughly and accurately, you need to start your day with an intention of mindfulness. This means you need to be aware of how you feel when you are involved in certain activities. For instance, as you are working on an activity, do you feel a sense of joy and satisfaction? Do you find that you are drawn to those types of activities? When you receive acknowledgement or recognition for what you are doing, are you doing something you really enjoy?

As you continue to reflect upon and evaluate your experiences, you are, in essence, confirming your talents and strengths. So rather than say, "Oh, it was nothing," when you are given praise for a job well done, take time to note what you were doing, how you were feeling, and what part was most fulfilling and satisfying for you.

Summary

My hope is that you have taken the time to really reflect and evaluate many aspects of your life, specifically, your talents and strengths. I encourage you to keep coming back to these first two steps (*Discover* and *Discern*) throughout the remainder of your journey. Keep assessing your path by tracking your experiences. Keep a record of your Good Day vs. Bad Day experiences, as this will continue to inform you as you progress along your journey. Continuing to assess your experiences will sharpen the clarity of your lens as you make choices for your future. In time you will know almost immediately if the options before you will lead you down a good path, especially a path with a heart.

As we wrap up *Discern*, take a moment to go to your MAP and answer these questions:

- What themes seem to surface as I reflect on my experiences?
- What sorts of activities have brought me the most joy and satisfaction?
- Which strengths and talents do I want to take with me into my future?

The insight you gain from *Discern* will continue to inform your Gifted Journey. We will build upon the foundation you have created for your future in the third step, *Dream*, where we will start to imagine all the possibilities and potential paths that lie ahead.

CHAPTER FOUR

Step Three: Dream

"May you have the wisdom to enter generously into your own unease to discover the new direction your longing wants you to take."

—John O'Donohue, "For Longing"

Imagine the Possibilities

In the first step of your Gifted Journey, *Discover*, you accumulated information about who you are through the lens of your experiences and the assessment exercises. During *Discern*, you reflected upon and evaluated those experiences that brought you true joy and happiness and where you felt strong and confident. Now it's time to face forward with anticipation of what lies ahead. It's time to imagine what could be. It's time to *Dream*.

As a child, did you ever dream about what you wanted to be when you grew up? Like most children, you may have dreamt of being an actor, or a singer, or an astronaut, or a teacher. When we are young, there are no boundaries. Our minds are free and the sky's the limit. When we are young, we have this amazing ability to imagine our futures with great confidence and courage. We have a conviction that we can do anything. Think back to those days. You may have even shared your dreams enthusiastically with others. Perhaps you knew exactly what you wanted to be when you grew up. My guess is that you felt great joy and exhilaration as you imagined yourself in those moments, and you shared your dream with others.

When my oldest son was about four, he was convinced that he wanted to be a garbage collector. I remember asking him why that seemed so interesting, and he enthusiastically shared how he loved to watch the trucks pick up the cans and dump them into the truck. Week after week, every Thursday at six in the morning, nose pressed against the window, he watched the whole process. And then, at around age six, his dream changed and he wanted to be a professional clown. Something about performing and making people laugh suited his personality to a T. At age ten, he wanted to be a cartoonist until he was asked by the drama teacher to try out for the spring musical. He did, and after his performance, as he listened to the applause from the audience, he found his calling. He stayed with acting through grammar school, high school, and then college, where he obtained his bachelor of fine arts. His dream led him to a number of off-Broadway opportunities, and today, at age thirty-four, he still spends time performing in community theater.

Our dreams can change over the years, but the important thing is to have a dream and to open up our minds to the possibilities instead of worrying about whether or not our dreams are feasible. Unfortunately, the older we get the more we are reminded that we need to "get serious," and, conversely, sometimes our dreams are censored at an early age. For instance, if as a child you ever shared a dream with an unimaginative adult, you were probably told, "You'd better have a backup plan," or, "If everyone could be an actor, Broadway would be littered with millions of people trying to get on stage."

Our own self-doubt coupled with those early voices can make the *Dream* step difficult but not impossible.

So what does it mean to truly dream? It means letting your mind envision a future where the best version of you is fully realized. It means removing all the barriers and silencing the internal voices that say, "I can't," "I shouldn't," "I don't know how," or, "It's just not possible." It means letting your mind expand and imagine all the possibilities. To truly dream is to form a mental image of something not yet present.

This process requires taking time to quiet your mind to let yourself think about what a life would look like if you were living your values and using your talents and strengths every day. This may require finding a quiet space where you can relax and close your eyes. I find that doing this soon after the *Discern* exercises helps to formulate those visions more easily. As you let yourself think about where you've been and what you're learning, it is then easier to imagine what your life would look like if you were to do those activities that you really enjoy on a more regular basis. It is important to listen to both your head and your heart. Visualize paths that would bring you joy and exhilaration. As those pictures come into your mind, capture them in your Gifted Journey MAP. The more time you spend intentionally thinking about the possibilities, the more you will find that the images will become clearer and more detailed.

Dream Exercise 1: Let Your Mind Explore

In this exercise, you will simply allow your imagination to expand. Find a quiet place where you're unlikely to be disturbed and close your eyes if that is helpful. Take one of the statements below and let your mind wander. Don't try to censor your thoughts; allow interrupting thoughts to float through your mind as you repeat the statement to yourself.

Imagine yourself in an environment:
- with people who encourage and inspire you
- where you are contributing tremendous value
- where you flourish and grow
- doing activities that utilize your talents and strengths

Dream Exercise 2: Determine Your Focus

As you think about the images that surfaced in the previous exercise, look for themes that arose. In this exercise, you will begin to envision the focus for your future. The following questions are meant to help lead you down that path. From there, we will create a Personal Vision Statement in the next exercise.

The following questions can help you envision your potential future paths. Take notes as images spring into your mind.

1. In what ways do I envision myself doing activities that make me feel strong and confident?

_____

_____

_____

_____

_____

2. In what environments do I envision myself thriving?

_____

_____

_____

_____

_____

3. In what ways do I envision that I am impacting the world around me?

_____

_____

_____

_____

4. In what ways do I envision myself following my calling and purpose?

_____

_____

_____

_____

_____

Perhaps one or two of these questions resonate with you more than the others. Follow the train of thought that surfaces and envision as many details as you can.

Dream Exercise 3: Create a Personal Vision Statement

In this exercise, you will create a Personal Vision Statement. A personal vision statement is a clear and succinct description of what you are doing once you are on your perfect path. It should define what your life will look like when you are using your full potential. It is an expression of what you want your life to encompass—a preferred future.

Your personal vision statement should be both aspirational as well as inspirational: aspirational because it helps define your desire for a fulfilling and satisfying life and inspirational because it motivates you to move forward. A vision statement acts as your North Star by illuminating your ultimate destination. Making important decisions without a vision statement is like driving in the dark without your headlights on.

Take a moment and reflect on the questions you answered in Exercise 2 and write a draft of your vision statement here:

_____

_____

_____

Your vision statement is like your resume

In my early years of being a career counselor and working in out-placement, I had the great pleasure of helping many people write their resumes. Unfortunately, many people think a resume should be a laundry list of everything they've ever done in their lives. This is like moving to a new home without ever considering which of your possessions are meaningful and will bring you joy in your new space. Resumes should feature the skills and experiences that highlight where you want to go—not where you've been. This requires envisioning your future and crafting a resume that serves as a roadmap, with only your talents and strengths leading the way to your final destination.

Like a carefully crafted resume, your personal vision statement should reflect who you want to be going forward.

Dream Exercise 4: Continue to Dream Your Way to Self-Actualization

In this exercise, you will firmly plant that dream into your conscious and subconscious. Abraham Maslow believed that once a person's basic needs are met (food, clothing, security, a sense of belonging), one can reach "self-actualization." Self-actualization is the need to be good, to be fully alive, and to live with purpose and meaning. This is why creating a vision of your future self can be a powerful step in your Gifted Journey.

To continue to firmly plant your vision in your brain, do the following:

- As you are in a relaxed state, getting ready to fall asleep, picture yourself in your ideal job, doing work you love in an environment where you flourish. Envision yourself with people, note your surroundings, listen for sounds, and capture what you see. Be mindful of your feelings of joy, satisfaction, and well-being.

Practice this visual imagery every day, and this will plant a seed that can open up your mind to new information and possibilities. Some call this the "law of attraction," which means that when we focus on something enough, we can actually attract people and experiences that will help us realize our goals.

Summary

In our busy, hyperconnected world, it can feel difficult at times to dream. This can be because many times our dreams are buried deep in our subconscious, and we simply never take the time to dig in and bring our subconscious thoughts to the surface. But these subconscious thoughts can be powerful trajectories into new possibilities. I've had many people who actively practice the art of dreaming tell me that new ideas will spring to mind and that they will hear or see things they otherwise wouldn't have noticed. I equate this phenomenon to what it's like when I buy a new car and suddenly all I see are those same cars on the freeway. That particular make and model was in the forefront of my mind. The same thing will happen when we acknowledge our subconscious thoughts and ideas and bring those into our conscious minds— suddenly the opportunities before us will become more obvious.

As we bring the *Dream* step to a close, take a moment to go to your MAP and reflect on these questions:

- What sorts of mental images continue to surface when I envision my path forward?

- What strengths do I envision using on a regular basis?

- What new ideas about my path have surfaced as a result of dreaming?

As your newly conjured images and possibilities bring clarity to your future choices, you are ready to move into the next step, *Design*, where you will begin to chart a course toward your ideal path.

CHAPTER FIVE

Step Four: Design

"Go where you are celebrated, not merely tolerated."

— Paul F. Davis

Creating a MAP for Your Future

In *Dream*, you spent time imagining a future where you are on a path that not only uses your strengths but is also fulfilling and enjoyable. The purpose of your dream is to inspire you to move forward with a sense of excitement as you prepare to create a tactical action plan in the fourth step, *Design*.

First, we are going to look at your overall focus, and from there we will look at specific goals and objectives.

To do this, we are going to complete the action part of your MAP. This will be your guide for your future, and its goal is to give you clear direction. It will incorporate much of the information you've gained and captured in *Discover*, *Discern*, and *Dream*. The key to this part of your MAP is that it's actionable. It requires your initiative and energy to make it realistic and to ultimately get you on your right path pointed toward your vision. In *Design*, all those questions you thought about in *Discern* and *Dream* start to take shape. The steps we will complete in *Design* for your action plan include:

- Creating your goal (destination)

- Developing your SMART objectives with timelines (milestones along the way)
- Creating your personal board of directors (people to take on your journey)

Design Exercise 1: Create Your Goal

In this exercise, you will use your vision statement from *Dream* to help you define a goal that is both actionable and attainable within the next five years. Some examples of your goal could be:

- To pursue a field of interest that will leverage my strengths and talents
- To enhance the current role I'm in by deepening my skills and talents
- To expand my current role by engaging in more cross-functional opportunities that leverage my strengths
- To move from my current role into something entirely different

My goal:

Design Exercise 2: Develop SMART Objectives to Reach Your Goal

In this exercise, you will develop three to five SMART objectives (or activities) that you will engage in to move you systematically toward your goal. SMART is an acronym for the following:

- **S**pecific – Be as specific as possible. What do you hope to accomplish and what will success look like? For example, you may choose to expand your network of contacts.

- **M**easurable – What will be your measure of success? For instance, if you want to expand your network of contacts, by how many?

- **A**ttainable – Make sure your goal is attainable and that you are able to do it within the parameters you set.

- **R**elevant – What makes this goal relevant? This is your WHY. In this example, it may be that a broader network will help identify possible paths to pursue for your future.

- **T**ime-bound – State a date when this objective will be accomplished. Try not to set it too far out in the future—a few weeks to a few months.

Take some time now to develop several SMART objectives based on your overall goal. Break each objective down into attainable milestones—activities that you can engage in within the next few weeks to a few months. Establish due dates for each objective and each milestone and mark these dates on your calendar.

SMART OBJECTIVE 1

_____

_____

_____

Due Date: _____

Milestone 1:_____ Due Date: _____

Milestone 2:_____ Due Date: _____

Milestone 3:_____ Due Date: _____

SMART OBJECTIVE 2

_____

_____

_____

Due Date: _____

Milestone 1: _____ Due Date: _____

Milestone 2: _____ Due Date: _____

Milestone 3: _____ Due Date: _____

SMART OBJECTIVE 3

_____

_____

_____

Due Date: _____

Milestone 1: _____ Due Date: _____

Milestone 2: _____ Due Date: _____

Milestone 3: _____ Due Date: _____

SMART OBJECTIVE 4

_____

_____

_____

Due Date: _____

Milestone 1:_____ Due Date: _____

Milestone 2:_____ Due Date: _____

Milestone 3:_____ Due Date: _____

SMART OBJECTIVE 5

_____

_____

_____

Due Date: _____

Milestone 1:_____ Due Date: _____

Milestone 2:_____ Due Date: _____

Milestone 3:_____ Due Date: _____

SMART OBJECTIVE 6

_____

_____

_____

Due Date: _____

Milestone 1: _____ Due Date: _____

Milestone 2: _____ Due Date: _____

Milestone 3: _____ Due Date: _____

Design Exercise 3: Create Your Own Personal Board of Directors

In this exercise, I want you to think of yourself as your own corporation and create a "board of directors" to oversee the running of your company, ensure that good business decisions are being made, and provide sound judgment.

Your personal board of directors should consist of people who have shown an interest in you and your future. They may be current or previous managers, trusted friends and colleagues, mentors, coaches, teachers, or past associates. They can be anyone you trust and you believe can give you the objective perspective we talked about earlier in *Discover*. As you move forward with your MAP, your board of directors will serve as both guides and sounding boards. It's important that you let each person know that he or she is a member of your board and explain what your needs are.

My Personal Board of Directors:

1. _____

2. _____

3. _____

4. _____

5. _____

6. _____

7. _____

Summary

The *Design* step can seem overwhelming. After all, you've gathered a lot of information, and now it's time to assemble all the pieces into an action plan. Below are some helpful suggestions that can help you put your plan into action right away and move you toward your ultimate goal:

- Most successful plans leverage opportunities that are readily available. How can you start to use your strengths and talents right where you are?

- Start building and nurturing a network of people in your life to see how they can be bridges to information and opportunities.

- Consider going to more conferences, lectures, and community functions that can help you grow and learn more about your area of interest.

- Pursue classes, certifications, and/or credentials that could lead you to the work that you really want to be doing.

As we bring *Design* to a close, take a moment to go to your MAP and reflect on these questions:

- How is my goal a reflection of my vision statement?

- How will my SMART objectives move me closer to my goal?

- Who will I ask to be on my personal board of directors and in what ways can they help and influence my path forward?

Next, we will look for tangible ways to bring your plan to life. Your journey from this point forward will be a planned series of experiences that will continue to inform you as you move toward your new future. You should view each new day as another opportunity to learn more and hone your plan. Each day is a gift waiting to be opened and discovered. It's at this point that I hope you realize that your renewed enthusiasm is the "gift" in *The Gifted Journey*.

In our next chapter, *Do*, we will define and execute the next logical step in your plan. It's time to take action!

CHAPTER SIX

Step Five: Do

"In my beginning is my end.

We shall not cease from exploration, and the end of all our exploring will be to arrive where we started and know the place for the first time.

What we call the beginning is often the end. And to make an end is to make a beginning. The end is where we start from."

—C.S. Lewis

Live the Life that was Always Intended Just for You!

If I could sit with you right now, in this moment, I would love to hear how this journey has been for you up until this point. What have you discovered? What sort of feedback have you received? What have you dreamed? Where are you headed now?

You began this process by delving deeper into who you are. From there, you took time to reflect on what all that information could mean and you solicited feedback from others. And you dreamt about what could be, perhaps recognizing that pull you feel in a certain direction or the call you feel compelled to answer. The design of your plan is taking shape and guiding you toward the new direction you now want to go. For some, like the quote above, you have affirmed what you already knew deep down inside. Perhaps this path is not necessarily new, but more of an affirmation of where you were meant to go all along—it is familiar and new all at the same time. Now it is a matter of trusting this path and growing more confident that this is the path that was designed for you from the beginning. Depending on your spiritual bent, you might feel this was the person you were always designed to be.

Truly putting this plan into action requires focus, energy, and motivation. Later in this chapter are some exercises designed to help keep your motivation high.

Expand Your Network by Building Bridges Regularly

From this point going forward, I encourage you to see every person you encounter as a potential bridge along your path. And just like bridges that span ravines and rivers, these folks can connect you with destinations that would otherwise seem out of reach. Many times, the right people can be immensely valuable bridges to other people, information, resources, and opportunities.

I've always said that we can't complete this process in a vacuum. We need people who are good listeners, good connectors, good cheerleaders, and good friends. People, many times, are going to be your best resources in this process, which is why I like to suggest investing in a good life coach or finding a trusted mentor.

A life coach can provide outside perspective and add an element of accountability and ownership. He or she can be an objective sounding board and shed new light on your path. A life coach can also help you set realistic goals and encourage you to think beyond what might not seem possible.

A mentor can be anyone with a level of expertise that you want to acquire and can be a great way to expand your network and get real-time information on developing your skills and knowhow. A great mentor is someone you trust and is a good listener. They should also be someone who knows that the mentor-mentee relationship is a two-way street. Many great mentors say they learn as much from this relationship as the mentee.

Take time to invest in building and enriching your connections. The following exercise can help in some of those first encounters. I have found that the more you make connections the easier it gets. Your connections can open doors to new information, new connections, and exciting possibilities. This can and should also be a reciprocal relationship, one in which you may be able to offer something in return.

Do Exercise 1: Connect with Others

Set up one coffee or lunch date with either a colleague, mentor, coach, or member of your personal board of directors each week. Consider the following topics for that time:

- Share the progress of your journey.

- Learn something new about them; be inquisitive.

- Share your interests and find places of common interest.

- Be a great listener; be sincere.

- Ask for other potential connections that they may be willing to introduce you to, based on your interests.

- Follow up with a thank you note or email and, if possible, attach a related article or item of interest to them.

If you are on the introverted side, this can be a little challenging. Take heart and be yourself. Don't feel you have to somehow become an extrovert. This is where being a great listener can really pay off. Be prepared to ask a few questions of personal interest and let the other person share. I find in almost every case I will walk away with invaluable information about that person and their areas of interest, as well as a bridge to help us stay connected.

Do Exercise 2: Revisit and Update Your MAP

As you continue to move down your path and learn more from your own experiences and your interactions with others, revisit your MAP on a regular basis. I like to suggest at least once a quarter and ideally once a month. Keep your MAP current as a living and breathing document.

As you review your MAP, ask yourself the following questions:

- What have I accomplished since the last review? What steps have I taken to get closer to my vision and goals?

- Who have I met with and what have I learned?

- What new skills have I acquired? Are they potential strengths? Potential weaknesses?

- What new learning have I invested in? What classes have I taken?

Do Exercise 3: Create a plan to be a Continuous Learner

In this exercise, identify the skills, knowledge, and experiences you need to continue to learn and grow and progress along your chosen path. Answer the following questions:

1. What subjects or topics would I most enjoy learning about?

_____

_____

_____

_____

_____

2. What clubs, groups, or associations would be beneficial to join?

_____

_____

_____

_____

_____

3. What are ways I can keep up on trends and future developments in my field of interest?

_____

_____

_____

_____

_____

Set your mind to learn something new as part of your ongoing growth and development.

The Road Not Yet Traveled: Keep Yourself Open to New Paths

Remember, _The Gifted Journey_ is a process. You may have perfect clarity regarding some aspects of your future path, while other aspects may remain fuzzy. You may know the work you want to do or the activities that will bring you joy, but you may not have found the environment. Here is where you need to think of every path as having some "off ramps" that allow you to explore the terrain, test out some activities, and determine if this path is leading you in the right direction. It is like traveling down the highway and seeing some points of interest at the next exit. Take the exit and determine if it is something you enjoy and want to revisit in the future or if it's something you can quickly dismiss as "been there, done that." One of the great advantages of *The Gifted Journey* is that by now you should feel more confident when it comes to making choices related to your future path. You should be able to discern what is best for you much quicker and in the moment.

Do Exercise 4: Reflect and Record Your Daily Experiences

Reflecting on the experiences you have each day is a valuable practice that can help keep you moving along the right path. You can use your MAP to record your thoughts.

At the end of each day, consider the following:

- Where did I use my strengths today?
- Where did I feel a sense of energy, joy, and/or satisfaction?
- Where did I feel drained or frustrated?
- Whom did I connect with and what did I learn?
- In what ways was I recognized or acknowledged for the value that I added?
- What did I learn today?
- What am I grateful for?

Again, these questions—answered every day—will continue to clarify and affirm who you are and where you are going. Use your answers to these questions to inform your future choices and to keep you headed in the right direction.

Be Good to Yourself Along the Way!

As you go through this process, it can be easy to forget to nourish your body along with your mind. Depending on your current situation, you may be feeling overwhelmed, stressed, or anxious. It is important to incorporate healthy activities that will take care of your body, mind, and spirit. A few ideas include:

1. Take a brisk walk every day. Just the activity of walking can help clear your mind and calm your soul.

2. Meditation is great for clearing your mind and relaxing your body. When I start my day in a quiet space and close my eyes and clear my mind, I am much more focused and calm throughout my day.

3. Treat yourself to an activity that brings you joy, whether it is gardening, reading, playing sports, bicycling, going to the gym, or visiting with friends. Do something that makes you feel good.

4. Get enough rest. Sleep is key to a healthy life and a calm mind.

5. Stay connected to others who make you happy. Surround yourself with those who love and support you.

Summary

Momentum is key in this ongoing process. Do one small thing each day to keep your journey ever present in your mind. As much as it is possible, wake each day with a mindset of excited anticipation for what the day will bring—what will be affirmed and what new discoveries will be made. This is truly your unique Gifted Journey. May it bring you to a place of contentment, happiness, joy, and satisfaction. May it make you ever mindful of the amazing individual you are and all you have yet to accomplish and contribute to the world.

As we complete the *Do* step, go to your MAP and reflect on these questions:

- What is one immediate activity I can do to put my plan into action?

- Who is one person I can connect with within the next week?

- What is one class or seminar I can sign up for that is in my area of interest?

- What is one habit I want to start or continue daily to keep me working on my plan?

CHAPTER SEVEN

Putting it All Together in 5-D

"This is the true joy in life, being used for a purpose recognized by yourself as a mighty one. Being a force of nature instead of a feverish, selfish little clod of ailments and grievances, complaining that the world will not devote itself to making you happy. I am of the opinion that my life belongs to the whole community and as long as I live, it is my privilege to do for it what I can. I want to be thoroughly used up when I die, for the harder I work, the more I live. I rejoice in life for its own sake. Life is no brief candle to me. It is a sort of splendid torch which I have got hold of for the moment and I want to make it burn as brightly as possible before handing it on to future generations."

— George Bernard Shaw

Staying the Course

Your Gifted Journey is comprised of five steps designed to work together in harmony—each step informing the next to generate a cycle of discovering, discerning, dreaming, designing, and doing exactly what you need to live a more satisfying life. To help you stay the course on your Gifted Journey, I'd like to do a quick review of the 5-D process and share some strategies for long-term success.

Discover – In this step, you thought about your past leading up to the present. You identified your values, motivated skills (strengths), a good day vs. a bad day, and your talents. You sought and (hopefully) received valuable feedback from those you trust regarding your abilities and strengths.

Discover strategies for long-term success:

- Continue to assess yourself regularly using both internal and external sources. There are many great assessments out there that can provide insight and language into who you are. While you have experienced a few of them in this book, there are others worth noting:

  - Myers-Briggs Type Indicator (MBTI) – Based on the theories and studies of Carl Jung and created by a mother-daughter team (Isabel Briggs-Myers and Katherine Briggs) as a way to make type theory accessible to individuals and groups, this personality assessment is widely used and is based on sixteen personality types and can help you understand your unique personality. The MBTI assessment can be found here: https://www.myersbriggs.org/my-mbti-personality-type/take-the-mbti-instrument/.

○ Instinctive Drive (The I.D. System) – This assessment reveals your innate drives and motivations and identifies what you need to be at your best both personally and professionally. The Instinctive Drive assessment can be found at: https://www.instinctivedrives.com/products.

○ StandOut Assessment 2.0 – Developed by Marcus Buckingham and his team at The Marcus Buckingham Company, this tool enables you to identify your top two StandOut roles out of nine possible. These "roles" determine "how you show up" in a given situation. This assessment can be very helpful to take in combination with the CliftonStrengths assessment. The StandOut assessment can be found at: https://www.tmbc.com/standout-2-0-assessment/.

○ VIACharacter Assessment – The VIA Institute on Character is a nonprofit organization dedicated to bringing the science of character strengths to the world through supporting research, creating and validating surveys of character, and developing practical tools for individuals and practitioners. The VIACharacter assessment can be found at: https://www.viacharacter.org/www/Character-Strengths-Survey.

• Continue to seek coaching feedback from trusted sources. The latest term is "feed-forward" coaching, which means looking for ways to continue to evolve your skills as you go forward on your journey. Mentors, coaches, and trusted colleagues can help provide insight needed to point you in the right direction.

Discern – In this step, you reflected upon and evaluated the recurring themes in your life and considered which experiences to take with you into your future.

Discern strategies for long-term success:

- Make a commitment to continue to seek insight about yourself as part of an ongoing process. Some great questions to answer periodically include:

  o What do I continue to affirm about myself as I reflect back on my past?

  o What new insights and knowledge am I gaining about myself?

  o How do I tend to interact with the world around me?

  o What feedback am I getting from others that sheds light on who I am?

  o How do I tend to respond in certain situations? What is that telling me about myself? My values? My strengths?

Dream – In this step, your imagination took center stage, and you created a visual representation of what a perfect path might look like for you.

Dream strategies for long-term success:

- Learn to be a daydreamer. Set aside ten to twenty minutes a day to sit or lie in a quiet space and envision yourself in your perfect environment.

- Keep a journal of the images that come up in your dreams. Note the specific environment, people, and activities. Be as specific as you can be.

- Share your dreams with others (preferably those who are good listeners). Sharing your dreams out loud can take them to another level of understanding and commitment.

Design – In this step, you began an action plan for your future—a plan with specific goals and strategies that will leverage the best of who you are.

Design strategies for long-term success:

- Keep your MAP up-to-date. Revisit and track your progress on a regular basis.

- Take time to acknowledge your accomplishments and completion of goals.

- Share your MAP with those who can help and support you with your goals.

- Keep your resume and social media sites up-to-date and highlight those abilities and strengths that you want to take with you going forward.

Do – In this step, you identified strategies that will keep you motivated and on the right path going forward.

Do strategies for long-term success:

- Commit to doing one activity each week that will help you grow and develop. Some suggestions:
  - Take a course (online, live, or on-demand)
  - Join a club or association
  - Read a book or article of interest
  - Take on a new activity
  - Find a mentor or life coach
  - Volunteer for a charity
  - Research new trends and opportunities
  - Listen to a podcast
  - Stay healthy

With these five steps, you now have a proven process to guide you toward a more fulfilling and rewarding life. Continue to revisit these steps from time to time on your journey and they will help you stay on course, particularly if and when you hit a bump in the road.

Course Correcting if You Hit a Roadblock

Change is one of life's stable constants, and there may very well be moments along your journey when life's perpetual evolution will land you in an unfamiliar and undesirable situation. For instance:

- You may suddenly have a new manager with a completely different style than yours.

- A company reorganization could force you into a position that doesn't play to your talents or strengths—or you could be out of a job completely.

- You may have thought you were on the right track, but suddenly you've lost your enthusiasm for the role you thought you wanted and the path forward isn't clear.

- You completed the five steps and created a realistic goal and action plan, but you haven't had any luck finding a job in your chosen career path.

A few strategies to consider:

- Reflect upon and evaluate what you are experiencing and how you are feeling. Capture your thoughts in your Gifted Journey MAP.

- Talk to people you trust. The act of verbalizing what you are feeling can help move you through the roadblock. Seek out a life coach, mentor, or trusted friend.

- Stay healthy and active as you contemplate your choices and paths, whether that means a brisk walk, a yoga class, a day walking on the beach, or a hike in the wilderness.

- Return to your Gifted Journey process and reflect on your *Discover* and *Discern* steps to remind you of your gifts and talents.

- Immerse yourself in the *Dream* and *Design* steps to help inform your plan forward.

Make Your Journey a Lifelong Continuum

Your journey is an ongoing and evolving process, and it is not over just because you have finished this book. Here are some ways to incorporate *The Gifted Journey* in your everyday experiences:

- **Continue to update your MAP.** Just like updates to the GPS in your car, you need to update your action plan on a regular basis. Look at your vision statement and SMART goals to keep you headed in the right direction.

- **Notice the road signs along the way.** In other words, take time to reflect at the end of each day. *The Gifted Journey* MAP can help you capture your reflections that you can later revisit.

- **Check your rearview mirror frequently.** Be aware of what is coming up behind you that could impact your journey. Are you staying ahead of emerging trends? What about the competition? Are you keeping your skills and expertise up-to-date?

- **When things aren't clear turn on your high beams.** Look down the road for future trends and opportunities. Find ways to proactively learn about your areas of interest. Invest in being a continuous learner.

- **Welcome trusted passengers on your journey.** The people in your life are key to helping you navigate the roadway. They can point out essential things you may have missed about yourself or your direction.

Enjoy Your Journey

Above all else, ENJOY your journey! Remember, your journey is uniquely yours. You are the only one who can determine which path is right for you. At the end of the day, reflect with a sense of gratitude for all those moments that either taught you something new, affirmed what you knew about yourself, or added clarity to your path.

In our final chapter, we will shift our focus from the Gifted Journey process toward what some call "a deeper longing." As you progress down your path, you may find that something is nudging you to move into an area of deeper purpose and meaning.

CHAPTER EIGHT

A Deeper Longing

The Longing

"Blessed be the longing that brought you here
And quickens your soul with wonder.
May you have the courage to listen to the voice of desire
That disturbs you when you have settled for something safe.
May you have the wisdom to enter generously into your own unease
To discover the new direction your longing wants you to take.
May the forms of your belonging–in love, creativity, and friendship–
Be equal to the grandeur and the call of your soul.
May the one you long for long for you.
May your dreams gradually reveal the destination of your desire.
May a secret Providence guide your thought and nurture your feeling.
May your mind inhabit your life with the sureness with which your
body inhabits the world.
May your heart never be haunted by ghost structures of old damage.
May you come to accept your longing as divine urgency.
May you know the urgency with which God longs for you."

—John O'Donohue, "To Bless The Space Between Us"

From Seeking to Serving

As you focus on your vision and goals and the progress you've made throughout this journey, you will find yourself, like others, gaining more confidence in who you are, intentionally using your gifts and talents in more meaningful ways, and experiencing more success and fulfillment.

At this juncture of the journey, you may, like many others, start to ask different and even deeper questions about where you are headed and in what ways you can contribute to the greater community. In my twenty-plus years of leading career development workshops, spiritual gifts retreats, and one-on-one coaching, it's quite common for people to ask, "So what's next?" Or, "How can I take what I love and use it in even more significant and meaningful ways?" Or, deep down they have a more profound unanswered question: "How can I better understand my true meaning and purpose in this life?"

Have you ever received a gift that touched you deeply? Something that had so much meaning that you brought it out every time someone came by, perhaps with the intention of sharing that joy with others? Perhaps you were even compelled to "gift" it to someone who expressed the same joy you were feeling?

This is a shift from being "self-focused" to being "other-focused," which simply means you will seek to share your gifts and talents in a new and intentional way that can tie to your sense of purpose and mission in the world. This can be a fundamental shift in the way you think, see, and operate in the world. My guess is that you've probably already experienced the feeling that you get when you shift your focus to others. Other-focused activities might include:

- Raising your children
- Caring for an aging parent
- Donating your time to a nonprofit organization
- Giving money to a local or national charity
- Joining a ministry as part of your faith community
- Mentoring a student or colleague
- Assisting others in need
- Raising money for a cause
- Running errands for someone homebound
- Visiting those who are sick

In my experience, when we put ourselves "out there" it can take on more of a "mission-driven" feel. I believe most people want that sense of making a difference in the world.

This is what I believe Bernard Shaw meant in his quote. It is the acknowledgment that who we are, our gifts, and our talents are meant to be given to others.

For most, this realization does not happen overnight; it's an evolutionary part of this process. In some cases, and depending on a person's spiritual belief system, they can literally feel drawn to this perspective. And for those who do go down this path it can be a life-changing experience.

Spiritual Gifts and Our Mission and Purpose

Back in the early 2000s I had just completed ten years in the career development field and was looking at my path ahead and wondering if there was more to life than what I was currently doing. I felt a tug to offer my skills in a bigger and more meaningful way. I decided to talk to the pastor at our local church. I remember asking him about bringing a career development process to our parish that would help members of the congregation figure out who they are and what they are meant to do. He mentioned that he had just heard of a new spiritual gifts workshop that was designed to help people assess and discern their spiritual gifts. Up until then, while I knew about spiritual gifts from the Bible and scripture, I was not aware that there was an assessment that was designed to help you discern your own spiritual gifts. I attended the workshop and was profoundly impacted—it took my career development experience to an entirely different and deeper level. I found that it dramatically shifted my perspective from being self-focused to other-focused. After we rolled it out in our parish, I found that many were as impacted as I was.

The process uncovered and affirmed a deeply held belief that we are all here for a larger purpose and that we all have the ability to use our gifts and talents in a positive and intentional way to impact the lives of others. It also brought certain scripture passages to life.

A few examples include:

> *"You formed my inmost being; you knit me in my mother's womb. I praise you, so wonderful are your works!"*
>
> —Psalm 139:13-14

> *"There are different kinds of gifts, but the same Spirit distributes them. There are different kinds of service, but the same Lord. There are different kinds of working, but in all of them and in everyone it is the same God at work."*
>
> —1 Corinthians 12:4

> *"We have different gifts, according to the grace given to each of us. If your gift is prophesying, then prophesy in accordance with your faith; if it is serving, then serve; if it is teaching, then teach; if it is to encourage, then give encouragement; if it is giving, then give generously; if it is to lead, do it diligently; if it is to show mercy, do it cheerfully."*
>
> —Romans 12:4-8

> *"As each one has received a gift, use it to serve one another as good stewards of God's varied grace."*
>
> —1 Peter 4:10

Each of these passages speaks of spiritual gifts given to us by our creator and that we should use these gifts to serve one another. Our spiritual gifts should not only inform our focus but also our mission in the world.

In fact, everything we've learned so far in *The Gifted Journey* relates to our unique and natural way of being. Our spiritual gifts work in direct harmony with our natural gifts and talents. Together they inform the "what" and the "how" of who we are and what we are ultimately meant to do. Our spiritual gifts give us a sense of our mission, our focus, and the ultimate impact we can make on the world. Our talents and strengths can inform how those spiritual gifts will be uniquely expressed.

Once we shift our mindset from seek to serve, it can influence our journey in the most profound ways. This mindset can influence all we are and all we do. Even when I teach my leadership classes, I like to emphasize the power of being a "servant leader."

Be a Light on the Journey for Others

This is the ultimate Gifted Journey—to realize that you are an incredibly unique gift to this world; that the world needs all you have to give it; and without you there will be a void that can never be filled.

Questions to consider:

- In what ways have I been using my talents, strengths, and gifts to impact the world around me?

- In what ways can I further donate my time and energy to help others who need my gifts and talents?

My Final Words to You

My wish for you is that you live your unique and powerful Gifted Journey. May you discover your ultimate power that is already within you, and may you stay true to your path. Trust your gut and your instincts to guide you where you want and need to go. May your life bring you the ultimate joy from knowing who you are and where you are meant to give of your abilities, talents, and strengths. May you never stop exploring the deeper meaning of your life. May grace, love, and light be with you all your days.

Many blessings on your journey!

Afterword

My Personal Gifted Journey Story

For me, the idea of traveling along a "gifted" journey has been a deeply personal and profound experience. I've spent twenty-plus years as a corporate career counselor, workforce development consultant, corporate trainer and facilitator, and senior leader. On my faith side, I've led large initiatives and conducted numerous workshops and retreats focused on helping individuals discover their God-given talents and strengths. All of these experiences have reinforced a few key themes. One is that as human beings we will never stop pondering the questions, Who am I? and, What am I meant to do with my life? The quick follow-up question is always, Once I figure out who I am, where do I go from here? As I've worked with countless individuals and become even more aware of my my own journey, my work has evolved into a passion to help others discover, develop, and affirm their journeys, and this passion continues to be the core of all of my work. On a personal level, what I teach others also guides me toward making certain choices in my career and has become my own personal testimony that it is possible to live a life full of meaning and purpose, once one understands how to make informed choices along the way.

As I reflect back on my journey, I recognize that I've made a lot of choices and taken a number of different paths—some that were great and some that were not so great. As my career progressed, I could see a pattern emerge: those not-so-great choices didn't align with the core of who I am, namely, my values and talents. Even though those choices may have led to some accomplishments, I didn't feel that deep sense of joy and satisfaction or a sense of value and contribution. At the time, as much as I now hate to admit it, I believe I made those choices for other tempting and socially desirable reasons such as prestige, ego, and money. However, in the end, I somehow knew that those choices compromised my very being.

The Seed was Planted

In Chapter One, I shared a story about a sales trainer who wore a bright red suit. She not only left a lasting impression on me; she planted a seed. I knew I wanted that seed to grow, but my manager at the time was less than encouraging. Fortunately for me, about a year later I was transferred to a more forward-thinking manager who actually believed in developing people.

During my first one-on-one, get-acquainted meeting with my new manager, she asked me what I could see myself doing in the future. I remember feeling hesitant and somewhat vulnerable. Should I share my deep-seated desire to move from sales to training? How would she receive this information? The mere fact that she asked me this question at all led me to trust her just enough to share that I wanted to pursue a career in the training field. When she asked why, I shared my story about the woman in the bright red suit. My manager pondered that for a moment while I held my breath. And then she said, "Then I guess we need to get you in front of people as often as possible. Have you ever thought of being an ambassador for the company?" She explained that an ambassador represented the company at tradeshows, conferences, and at annual meetings, all of which would require making brief presentations. As she was explaining the role, I felt in that moment a sensation of true joy, as if that seed (which had been lying dormant) was now taking root and starting to grow. For the next couple of years, I was an ambassador for the company. I made presentations, learned to use PowerPoint, and learned how to speak to small and sometimes very large crowds. In 1986 this same manager was promoted to a training role at the company headquarters, and within a month she brought me with her and I ended up in my very first "official" training role. As I've told many groups since then, I owe my career to this woman!

Over the years as my career progressed, I had many opportunities to follow my path and hone my training skills. I have been fortunate to work for both for-profit and nonprofit companies in the field of career transition and development. As a result, and over time, I have witnessed a significant shift in the way people view careers, work, and life.

For the past thirty years, buyouts, layoffs, and reorganizations have gradually become the norm—a trend that has significantly impacted how the workforce views job security. In fact, the term "job security" seems destined for extinction. Lacking any sense of loyalty to their current employers, people change jobs frequently. Companies are scrambling to hold on to their best and their brightest. Coaching practices are springing up like wildflowers and becoming a core competency inside many organizations, all in an effort to cultivate an engaged workforce and retain key talent.

A New Paradigm Continues to Emerge

In the mid-nineties, some groundbreaking studies underscored the need for employees to take control of their own careers.

The Career Action Center, a nonprofit organization, had just published a white paper in the Harvard Business Review titled, "Toward a Career Resilient Workforce."[3] The article described the tension between the employer and employee and this new world of work. It highlighted the need for employees to be "career self-reliant" and for organizations to build a resilient workforce. The article identified six characteristics of career-resilient individuals: they are self-aware, values-driven, dedicated to continuous learning, future-focused, connected, and flexible. In 1994 the idea that employees were no longer being "taken care of" and that they needed to drive their own careers was truly groundbreaking for most organizations. The Career Action Center became an overnight sensation, setting the world of organizational career development in motion. I joined the CAC during the launch of a consulting arm and started working with one of their largest clients, Hewlett-Packard. Over the next few years I helped implement a career development initiative to help individuals who were in "redeployment," which meant that their roles were being eliminated and their new "jobs" were to find other jobs within the organization. Today, as we look back, Hewlett-Packard was one of the first large companies to become a leader in this area, with other Fortune 100 companies soon to follow. During that time my dream had been realized.

In 2000, I launched my own company, The Moore Group, Inc., with a mission and vision to help individuals live with purpose and passion. Today, our primary focus is to help people find what brings them joy, peace, and happiness. In 2008, I became co-founder of the Catholic Strengths and Engagement Community. It's a national, mission-driven organization with a goal to assist faith-based organizations in building vibrant and engaged communities that help individuals discover their God-given talents and gifts.

Today, I speak nationally at a number of conferences. I also teach employee and leadership development programs on a regular basis at several Silicon Valley organizations.

As I reflect on my journey, I can look back to my first job and the vulnerable young woman I used to be, and I thank God I decided to pursue my dream.

One Last Story ...

A number of years ago, my husband and I went snow skiing. I remember standing in line to purchase our ski lift tickets, and the couple in front of us had a boy who looked to be about four years old. A melting patch of snow had formed a stream of water that snaked its way down the path we were standing on, and it caught the boy's attention. While his parents were engaged in deep conversation with another couple in line, the boy began assembling twigs on top of leaves to send down the stream. His makeshift boats would invariably tip over, spilling the twigs. But the failed attempts only fueled his determination. This went on for a while, completely unnoticed by his parents. As I continued to watch this little guy, I started to see a future engineer or someone with the determination to solve great problems. I watched as he scouted out bigger leaves and different sized twigs and tried different combinations, each time getting closer to his goal of sailing his invention all the way down the stream. I was also aware that his parents were oblivious to the miracle happening right in front of them. And then, the little boy put together the perfect combination of leaves and twigs, and his invention floated effortlessly the whole length of the stream! His face lit up with surprise and delight. But his excited shouts of "Mom," and, "Dad," as he pointed to the stream went unacknowledged as his parents continued their conversation. He approached his parents with excited enthusiasm and started pulling on his mom's sleeve. "Mom, Dad, you have to see what I just did!" he told them. "Not now; we're talking," was their dismissive response. I felt my heart sink, as his little shoulders slumped over and a look of total disappointment appeared on his face. I immediately went to him and leaned down and told him how wonderful his invention was. I told him that I had watched how hard he had worked and how excited I was to see the success of his efforts. He just shrugged his shoulders and looked down at the ground. I knew in that instant mine were not the accolades he was hoping for, but maybe he remembered my words later, and maybe my words made a difference.

We all have opportunities every day to recognize and acknowledge the gifts and talents in others, and I hope you will give the gifts of affirmation and attention as you travel your Gifted Journey.

Taking us where we need to go

Stepping stones
guide our paths
across unsettled waters
as the mysterious future unfolds,

prepared for us as we walk
prepared by us
in our walking,

the pale ground beneath our feet,
the next step,
the unknown before and within us;

the wales and wiles of the interior and exterior interact,
each step trusting the ground will hold,
the path made and, in the making,
will take us where we need to go.

—W. Craig Gilliam, 2015 (rev. 2018)

HELPFUL RESOURCES

StrengthsFinder 2.0, Tom Rath

Strengths Based Leadership: Great Leaders, Teams and Why People Follow, Tom Rath and Barry Conchie

Living Your Strengths, Albert L. Winseman, Curt Liesveld, and Donald O. Clifton

SMART Goals: The Ultimate Goal Setting Guide, Jacob Gudger

The Owner's Manual for Values at Work, Pierce J. Howard

Do What You Love, The Money Will Follow: Discovering Your Right Livelihood, Marsha Sinetar

To Build the Life You Want, Create the Work You Love: The Spiritual Dimension of Entrepreneuring, Marsha Sinetar

StandOut 2.0: Assess Your Strengths, Find Your Edge, Win at Work, Marcus Buckingham

Soar With Your Strengths, Donald O. Clifton and Paula Nelson

The Language of Blessing, Joseph Cavanaugh III

CliftonStrengths Assessment: www.gallupstrengthscenter.com

About the Author

Stephanie Moore is a Gallup-certified strengths coach with more than two decades of experience in leadership development, career consulting, and executive coaching. Her broad industry experience includes the telecommunications, high tech, biotech, manufacturing, healthcare, finance, nonprofit, and career development sectors.

As a strengths-based practitioner, she has used her unique blend of expertise, passion, and spirituality to help thousands of people discover more fulfilling and rewarding career paths. She has designed and currently delivers the highly successful and comprehensive development courses, *Strengths-Based Development* and *Strengths-Based Teams*, to organizations, universities, and associations across the globe.

Since launching The Moore Group, Inc., in 2000, Moore has provided her consultation and facilitation expertise to a number of leading-edge organizations, including Cisco Systems, NetApp, eBay, LinkedIn, SalesForce, Genentech, Oracle, Texas Instruments, Stanford University, and Lucille Packard Hospital.

In 2008, she cofounded the Catholic Strengths and Engagement Community, a 501(c)(3) nonprofit that helps faith-based leaders build vibrant and engaged communities by helping individuals discover their God-given talents and gifts.

She is a native of Northern California and attended St. Mary's College in Moraga, California, where she earned her bachelor's degree in psychology. She is also a graduate of the School for Pastoral Ministry through the Diocese of Oakland.

She is currently developing a series of retreats and workshops that follow *The Gifted Journey* process.

Endnotes

1.   Cooperrider, D.L. et. al. (Eds), *Lessons from the Field: Applying Appreciative Inquiry*, Thin Book Publishing, 2001, page 12.

2.   http://www.businessdictionary.com/definition/values.html

3.   Collard, Betty, and Robert Waterman, "Toward a Career Resilient Workforce," Harvard Business Review (1994).

Made in the USA
Lexington, KY
06 October 2018